TIGERFISH!

A Photojournal from Two Years of Fishing on West Africa's Niger River

A sometimes humorous look at sport & traditional fishing, and local hunting practices in Mali, West Africa

***

Text and Photos Copyright 2013 – M. Sid Kelly

(Additional photography by J. Anne Kelly, G. Lasine Doumbia, and Adama Sogoré)

ISBN-13: 9780692023846 (Galactic Pool Publishing)

***

"Kelly has produced a book of class about fishing in a region where few of us are likely to get the chance to visit. ...a mixture of absolute self-effacing honesty and intelligent insight." ~ **Paul Little, Little Ebook Reviews**

This book is also available in full-color as a free ebook if you have purchased the paperback through Amazon.com

Foreword

This photo journal documents various fishing and hunting activities that we experienced in Mali, West Africa from 1992 to 1994, and during my return trip in 2005.

The journal opens with **sport fishing**. If you enjoy fishing, there's nothing quite as exciting as showing up in a mysterious land to fish for who-knows-what and learning the water from scratch. And if it happens to be a river reach in Africa where nobody but you has a rod and reel, and there are tigerfish, Nile perch, and "stunning" electric species... Well, it can be a lot of fun.

The second section of this book is about the **traditional community fishing** events that take place on ponds, shallow lakes, and old channels of the Niger River's floodplain in southern Mali. These events were the best way to see the full variety of fish and experience mass fishing excitement. The group fishing events may seem like free-for-alls at first glance, but there is wise management and some serious "magic" involved. I try to explain.

The third section of this book is about the Somono **commercial fishers** that worked and lived on that reach of river. We became good friends with one family of fishers, and they encouraged me to document some of their activities.

I shot the crisper-looking of the 100-plus images with a Nikon Coolpix 995 digital camera during my return trip in 2005. The remaining pictures are taken from 35mm slides and negatives, or are scanned from prints, and were shot with a Canon point-and-shoot or a Pentax-copy with a telephoto lens.

And the final section documents two fire hunts that took place on the river floodplain in 1993.

This is the Niger River in Mali near the border with Guinea on Christmas Day 1993. You can tell from the smoky haze that the dry season's grass fires have begun.

But during the rainy season between approximately June and October, the river can inundate the floodplain as far as two miles beyond the far bank. Many fish will have moved with the water into temporary and permanent lakes and ponds. And then the rain stops and the river drops.

Some of the fish in these ponds are permanent residents – they live there year-round throughout their entire life cycles. Other fish are temporary visitors that spawn and rear in the ponds before moving to the main river as they mature. And some fish are opportunistic predators that move in during the flood season. Once the river drops though, some of the temporary visitors fail to make it back to the river.

In any event, during the dry season, these ponds are full of all sorts of fish. And when the river is low it is possible to catch them...

The text references colors in some of the pictures. A full-color ebook is available for free through the MatchBook program if you purchased the paperback through Amazon.com.

M. Sid Kelly – May 2013

***

Table of contents

SPORT FISHING

I rode my bike across the floodplain as soon as the river had dropped enough. I didn't feel so dumb in making THAT decision...

Since this was my first fishing effort on the Niger River, I just headed directly to the closest accessible reach. I ended up at a spot above a mid-channel island. The water was a little bit slower and deeper than it was just upstream and downstream, but it didn't look that great.

Still, I'm a California boy, so what do I know? I figured I should just cast and let Africa teach me what a good spot is...

So I tied on my favorite when-in-doubt lure – a chartreuse-sparkle curly-tail grub – and winged it out there as far as I could. It landed in three or four feet of water flowing over rippled sand. I let it sink and then bumped it along the bottom as it drifted in an arc downstream.

The first bite was distinct – a nice peck-peck in the rod handle. I set the hook and the fish felt heavy on my light tackle, but there wasn't much of a fight. This fish was not freaking out. Sometimes that's the first clue that you've hooked a big fish.

But where I come from, we always considered it bad luck to catch a fish on the first cast. And not only was this my first cast of the day, it was my first cast on an entire continent! I respect this superstition as nothing more than a fun tradition, which is good because I was a little bit afraid of hippos and crocodiles at the time. But this fish on my line made my newbie-self forget about potential dangers for a few minutes.

The fish continued to trace the original arc of the jig downstream and toward shore. I gained line easily though, and wondered whether I'd hooked something other than a fish. It reminded me of accidentally hooking a Dungeness crab in the ocean back home.

Then when I got this mysterious thing in close enough to see, I thought it must be a child's toy ball. But then I thought it must be some kind of turtle – but I thought this only briefly because I went back to thinking it was a water-logged bouncy ball again.

The dang thing really looked like a ball. It was white with yellow and dark brown stripes. And it was about the size of a softball. I wasn't looking for eyes or fins at that point – I was calculating the odds of a ball sinking in this river and getting hooked by me. And then I saw fins and eyes, and it dawned on me – it was a puffed-up pufferfish! Almost two-thousand river miles from the ocean…

A fahaka pufferfish on a different day

***

Mister fish biologist with a degree in marine biology

didn't know that about two dozen puffer species around the world live entirely in fresh water. I must have been absent on pufferfish day in fisheries class…

Now I know that this was a fahaka pufferfish (*Tetraodon lineatus*). I at least knew enough to be aware that you shouldn't eat puffers, no matter where they come from. And that's why I hadn't seen them in the markets.

But that doesn't mean you can't play with them, right?

It had typical pufferfish teeth that could take out a chunk of my flesh like a cookie-cutter, so I handled it carefully. I dug a pool in the sand next to the river deep enough for the fish to submerge in. But the puffer had expelled all of its water and had re-filled itself with air. Now it really was like a toy ball. It just floated there on the surface up-side-down.

But after a few seconds, it un-puffed itself and sank into the pool. It just sat there on the bottom, right-side-up and waving its pectoral fins. So I poked it (gently) until it filled up with water again. Coolest thing ever… But I let it go pretty quick because I had some more fishing to do.

Then on the second cast I hooked up with a tigerfish. Don't get too excited yet – it was about as big as a magic marker pen. I had seen tigerfish in the market, but this was my first live one in hand. I'm not sure whether I'd rather be bitten by a pufferfish or a tigerfish. But tigerfish dentition definitely looks more terrifying than the beak-like teeth of a puffer.

The remarkable thing about a tigerfish mouth, besides the teeth, is that the upper jaw is hinged. So they can open their mouth very wide and snap it like a bear trap. Their upper and lower teeth interlace when they bite, so they can take clean chunks from other fish that are too big to swallow whole. So I carefully played with this guy a little too before letting it go.

That would be the last edible fish I let go in Mali…

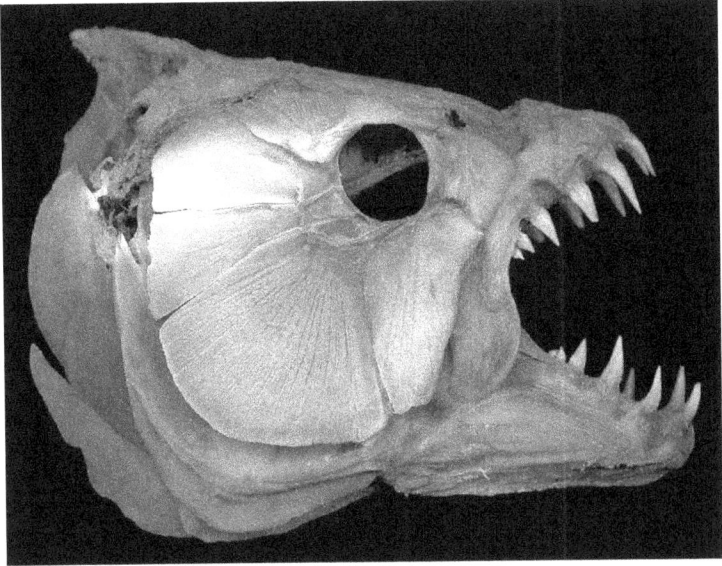

Tigerfish skull showing hinged upper jaw

***

But back to the beginning…

The big beautiful upper Niger River is full of amazing fish. Where we were going to be living was a wide meandering sand-bed river. And there are no dams large enough to impact downstream flows in the watershed above this location. So the river "behaves" naturally. Its floodplain is alive and well. There are very few rivers of this size that still function as natural channels. This is the only one I've ever seen.

So imagine how dumb I felt when I got to Mali for a two-year stay without any fishing gear. I had chosen to party and screw around during the weeks after I graduated instead of doing useful research about this river where I was going to live for two years. (These were pre-World Wide Web days, of course.)

But, yeah, it was a dumb decision on my part. I claim this as my official excuse though: The stupid Peace Corps packing list.

It turns out that you can buy most of the essentials in Mali pretty easily, so it wasn't necessary to follow the Peace Corps list very closely. But you can't easily (at least not in 1992) buy a rod and reel. I did find some big hooks and 100-pound test line in the capital city Bamako, but nothing that would put the "sport" in sport fishing.

Our Peace Corps training facility was right on the river, and the local markets were full of fantastic fish. Then I found out that our home village was going to be right on the most beautiful reach of the river in the country. Dumb, I felt.

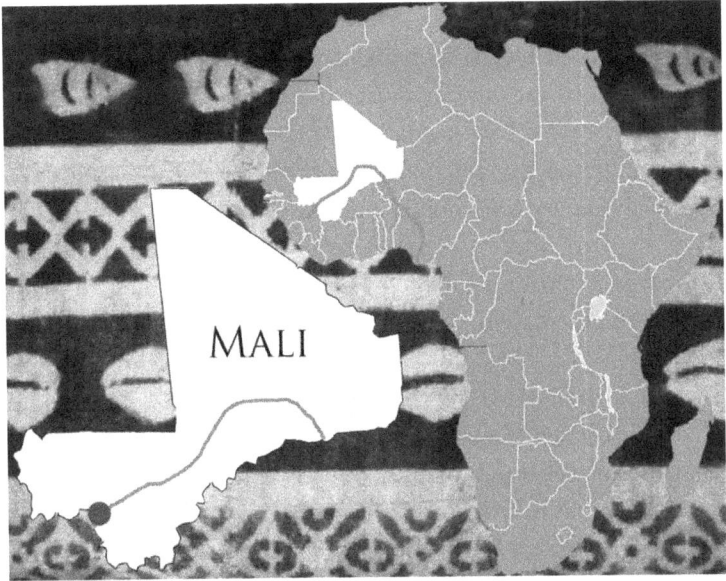

Maps showing approximate course of the Niger River through Mali and Africa. The river runs from south-west, to north-east, and then curves south to the ocean. The red dot near the headwaters is where this story takes place. (I drew the river on there myself, so don't rely on this for a geography exam.)

***

And to make things worse, there was a guy in my Peace Corps training group who HAD brought a rod and reel. He wasn't even a fisherman. He was just smart.

We didn't have a lot of free time during training, but I accompanied this smart guy and a mutual friend down to the river one evening to watch them fish. One of them caught a small "African pike" – a fish in the same family as tigerfish, but not quite that impressive in the tooth department. They had fun, but I came away feeling more than a little jealous.

But by the time we finished our three months of training, the rainy season had begun, the river had risen, and fishing opportunities at my new village were over for the year anyway. So I had time to write home and ask my folks to send a catalog so I could try and order some gear. When the catalog finally arrived and I made my order, I felt like a kid writing to Santa Claus. I ordered approximately this:

- A 6-foot, two-piece spinning rod
- A small spinning reel
- Several spools of 10-pound-test line
- A hundred or so jig heads
- A variety of bare hooks, swivels, split-shots, egg sinkers
- Plastic curly-tail grubs in black, white, and chartreuse
- A half-dozen spinners
- A few clear plastic bubble floats
- A big top-water plug (didn't catch anything)
- And some wire leaders

The postal service to and from Mali was reliable, but package delivery was VERY slow. It was common for packages to arrive that were meant for volunteers who had completed their service months before. Their replacements always appreciated the windfall M&Ms though.

And the catalog company wouldn't mail directly to Mali. So I sent the order to my Mom and worried that I'd never get the gear in time. I got it a lot sooner than I expected though...

Nile perch

***

The getting-of-the-gear started when I received a letter from a kid I knew in junior high school. She was coming to Mali! Not only did Christine R. bring my tackle order, she also brought a block of cheddar cheese. She had heard that J. Anne and I were in Mali, and she contacted my family.

They shared our letters full of grief about bringing all the stupid stuff on the Peace Corps packing list, and not bringing the most important stuff – like cheese and tackle. Christine was so grateful for the indirect advice via my letters, that she was happy to carry the gear in place of the dumb stuff Peace Corps had told her to bring.

Not only did she speed things up immeasurably, but it also avoided me having to pay import duties (which would only have funded the delay). So the heroic Christine R. from back-in-the-day arrived with everything I needed to start the fishing season with plenty of time to spare.

Gratuitous tigerfish teeth

***

Back at the river… After catching and releasing that first softball-sized pufferfish and pencil-thin tigerfish, I made a few more casts in the same area without another bite. I would come to learn that whenever I caught a tigerfish in a spot, that spot would shut down.

This early in the dry season, the river was still too high for easy access up and down that reach. So I went back to the village before it got too late and imaginary animals with big teeth came out... (Of course, it was the biters WITHOUT teeth that were the real problem.)

When I got back to the village after that first effort, everyone in my Malian family was excited to find out how I'd done. I told them about the puffer, and learned that its name in the Bambara/Malinké dialect of the area is *dodo*. They got a good laugh out of me catching a *dodo*. From then on, if I ever wanted to get a laugh from someone all I had to say was, "I went fishing and I caught a *dodo*."

However, they didn't laugh when I casually mentioned the tiny tigerfish I'd let go.

It didn't matter that the tigerfish was about as big as my middle finger. Size wasn't even a relevant consideration. I had thrown back a fish while my wife was telling everyone that the women should eat more fish when they are pregnant.

I pantomimed to them that I'd be thrown in jail in America for keeping a fish that small. But I also promised that I'd never do it again.

The next day I went back to the same spot and caught a Nile perch and then another, slightly bigger, tigerfish. The Nile perch jumped, and it felt a heck a lot like catching a largemouth bass in the San Joaquin River back home. And my Peace Corps service was quickly changing from "the toughest job you'll ever love" to "the best free time you'll ever have"! These two very exciting fish can be seen in the picture below where I look more maniacal than I am in real life.

Maniacal admiration of a small tigerfish

***

After stopping at home so J. Anne could take my picture, I went to deliver the fish to the pregnant women in my adoptive family. On the way there with the two fish strapped to my bike rack, I came up behind an old man and greeted him as I passed. He saw the fish and called out – asking if I had caught them. He couldn't believe it. When I took leave of him, he said, "*E DONSO!*"

This phrase means "YOU HUNTER!" and is a

benediction that one gives to real hunters. So I thought he was just teasing the American – a favorite pastime in the village. However, that exchange felt pretty cool to me, and other people took it up as a way to greet me sometimes. At least they had something to say instead of "May the gods fix your reproductive health!"

Just to show that I was legal – my 1994 Mali sport fishing license.

***

And then at work… The entire Malian student-body went on strike and the government was forced to cancel a year-and-a-half of school. The reasons for the student strike were complicated and were related to a recent military coup, but, yes, the students can do that there.

But from week to week the teachers and I didn't know

whether schools would re-open, so I went through the motions like I had a job. I ended up just hanging out with teachers who were going through the motions too – and not getting paid. We drank tea, ate kola nuts, talked about Mali and California, played foosball on an awesome hand-made foosball table, and entertained ideas about all the great things I was gonna do once they were "allowed" to work with me again.

So I effectively had no job of my own (not complaining), and acted as J. Anne's health education assistant (which I think was far more useful than re-training school teachers who didn't want to be re-trained anyway).

I was a man who had been married for five years and was "unable" to have children – and who was his busy wife's assistant and cook. I was a curiosity, but that's all. Until now.

Nile perch

***

Seriously, being able to consistently go out and bring back meat gave me way more credibility than anything else I could think of doing – besides fathering twelve kids and growing a year's supply of food, perhaps. Plus, I came up with this great idea: I'd give the pregnant women extra protein and hope that their babies were bigger and healthier – like J. Anne was teaching. This would show the fathers that they should buy fish instead of cigarettes, right?

This may be a case of motivating reasoning on my part, but it seemed like it worked. One of my friends quit smoking after his wife had a huge baby. And this was after having their previous baby be born underweight and surviving less than a week.

The rest of the village saw this big healthy baby too. So I eventually stopped feeling guilty and wimpy. (Yeah, I know one big healthy baby is not conclusive data, but, right or wrong, swapping your cigarettes for fish can't be a bad thing.)

When the river had dropped enough to open up better access, I went out for the purpose of scouting better fishing spots. I spent all day going upstream. I didn't find any honey-holes, but I had some success as I trudged along.

Yes, I caught a *dodo*. (Laughing now would be appropriate.) And I caught a couple of tigerfish – each about as big as a bratwurst. But the coolest fish I caught came on a bad cast.

I landed a spinner right against the bank in about an inch of water. As I reeled it in to cast again, a big half-circle wake turned toward it. A *Tilapia* nailed the spinner in water that was shallower than its body was deep. I think the *Tilapia* was on a nest. This was the first fish that pulled some drag from the reel. It reminded me of catching a really big North American sunfish – as if its flat body shape helped create resistance to the water as it fought.

While on the way back home, I noticed a bird that seemed to be following me through the riparian forest. It was a

Senegal coucal that was interested in me for some reason. I set one of the sausage-sized tigerfish on the ground and backed away. The coucal pounced on the dead fish and took off with it. (I didn't tell anyone that I gave their fish to a bird.) Anyway, I always liked those birds. They are in the cuckoo family and reminded me of road-runners with nice mellow whoot-whoot-whoot calls that they made outside our house almost every morning.

A *Bagrus* catfish

***

Then a few days later I spent the afternoon exploring downstream. The first good hole I found, which wasn't very far away, turned out to be my best Nile perch hole. But the first fish I caught in there was something other than a Nile perch.

This fish was apparently holding in the sand riffle just above the drop-off into the hole. It was one of those times where you come to realize that there's a fish on the other end of the line, rather than being startled by a bite.

The fish turned and dropped down into the hole, and I ran along the sand bank since I knew I wasn't going to be able to drag the fish back up into the riffle. When I got it to shore I saw a very flat head with a big mouth and long whiskers. It was a *Bagrus* catfish that weighed about five pounds. A guy from my village is holding one like it in the picture above. (But mine was bigger. I swear…)

I continued fishing that hole and caught a couple of Nile perch that were about two pounds each. I walked downstream about a half mile looking for another hole. I didn't find anything and it was getting late, so I decided to head home.

As I was walking back upstream, I met a Somono fisherman who didn't know there were any Americans living nearby, so he was pretty surprised. He was even more surprised that I had caught the three fish.

I showed him my gear, including the plastic grubs and jig-heads that I'd caught the fish on. I gave him some lures and he gave me two *bindamu* fish – a carp-like fish whose name means "grass eater" in Malinké.

And then as I was riding home I took a short detour to look at one of the floodplain ponds at twilight. As I approached the shore I stumbled right into the camp of two guys who were probably smugglers or fugitives, according to the blacksmith family. The men seemed much more shocked than me, however.

I gave them the two *bindamu* fish, which appeared to be the only food they had. The fish gift made them really happy – that and maybe because I wasn't some sort of special agent out to get them. I still wonder what they thought of the encounter.

Even after giving away two of the fish, I still came home with quite a big stringer that day. I felt like I was becoming a useful member of society...

Fish-on at my favorite spot

***

Then one day Adama Sogoré, one of the young Somono fishermen that I'd recently met at our Friday market, came to my door. He wanted to see me catch a fish with my impossibly small rod and reel, and he offered to take me into a deep tributary channel that could only be reached by boat. In my broken Malinké I said, "Hell yeah!" Thus began the friendship with the commercial fishers that I talk more about in the final section of this book.

Adama Sogoré setting a gillnet

***

So a couple of days later Adama, with his younger brother and a friend, took me to the mouth of a long winding channel in their wooden canoe. The deepest water in this stretch of the Niger River was at the confluence of this tributary – called *Le Fié*.

We all agreed that this confluence seemed like a good spot to try before we went up the channel. So I rigged-up with the reliable chartreuse grub and demonstrated a cast. I took a few casts and then offered to let them try. But no, they wanted to see me catch something. We were all hoping for a big Nile perch, of course. But they all agreed that my pole and line were too small for that.

These guys all had experience with monofilament line, and it showed in their ability to use it in a new application. Even though none of them had cast with sport tackle before, they were much better at it than the farmers and other people who tried to use my gear. They knew how to handle monofilament.

But for now they just watched and scrutinized. They seemed to agree with each other about a bunch of other things I didn't understand. I showed them that I was going to try a slower retrieve with the jig on the bottom. They, of course, all agreed that it was a good idea.

So I showed them the slack in the line to indicate that the jig was on the bottom. Then I lifted it to show how I was going to work it back to the boat very slowly while bouncing it along. But as soon as I lifted it, the jig stopped dead.

I could tell right away that it was a strong fish against my set-up. And I knew how to say "FISH ON!" in Malinké. I had even rehearsed it, silently, so I'd be fluent if I ever needed it. So I fluently shouted, "JEGE BE!"

Luckily we were in open, snag-free water. I REALLY didn't want my too-small line to break. The fish surged a few times – just enough to pull some drag. But it didn't run as much as it just bull-dogged back to the bottom. I pantomimed how the zzzzt-zzzzt sound was the reel's drag preventing the line from breaking, but I think they had already figured that out.

I expected it to be a catfish of some kind. And I was sure it wasn't a *dodo*, so that was reassuring – wouldn't want to get laughed at…

I was really happy when I saw that it was a new species for me – and one I didn't expect to catch.

An electric elephantfish, ouch!

***

It was the larger of several local electric African elephantfish (*Mormyrus rume*) – the one in the picture above. As you can see, it was hooked under the snout rather than in the mouth.

The various species of African elephantfish have a narrow base to their wide tail, which looks like a great place to grab them. Like *dodo*-day in fisheries class, I must have been absent or asleep on African elephantfish day too.

Anyway, I have that sheepish grin on my face due to the shock I received when I tried to lift this fish from the water by its tail. Yes, that's where the electric organ is located – right there on that perfect handle.

It hurt – a lot. It felt like my forearm had been slapped by a cricket bat. It was sore for a week, and my face never recovered. Adama and his friends probably haven't recovered from laughing either.

I wondered why they hadn't warned me. But maybe they had, and I just didn't understand.

I was beyond thrilled, but I tried to keep my cool. I told Adama that it was his turn now that I'd demonstrated how to do everything. They tried. However, Adama and his friends couldn't catch a fish with my pole even though it looked like they were getting the hang of casting it.

In fact, many fishermen, farmers, blacksmiths, teachers, and cattle herders eventually tried and failed. I really wanted someone to hook up with a fish on my rod and reel, but they couldn't even catch a *dodo*. At least maybe it prevented them from thinking that my fancy gear could catch fish with no skill required from the fisher.

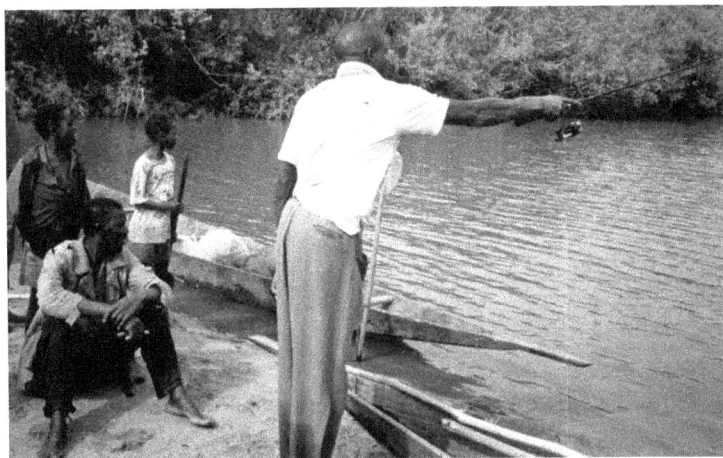

Another Somono fisherman getting skunked

***

The most self-conscious I felt about my fancy gear was on the day I found my second best Nile perch hole. This hotspot was an undercut bank on the main river channel just downstream from the little fishing village where Adama lived. There was an opening between a couple of small trees where I could cast from. I was about to make a short flip into what looked like a great spot. But then I heard voices coming from in the trees just behind me. There were three old men from my village mucking around in a large puddle.

They had built a mud dam across the middle of the puddle, and they were using a gourd to scoop all of the water from one side into the other. They completely dewatered one side and found nothing in it. Then they broke open the dam and let the water drain back to the other side – one of them keeping his hands in the gap in case a fish went through.

Then they plugged the dam again and scooped out the

water on the other side. They seemed to be enjoying the work, and I guess having me there for laughs probably helped. Plus I think there might have been some gambling going on.

In the second half of the puddle they found a banana-sized walking catfish. They seemed satisfied – especially the guy who I think won the bet. Now they wanted to see how my fishing gear worked. I showed them the set-up, and they agreed that my pole was too small.

I flipped the jig into the hole and hooked up with a three or four pound Nile perch. The old men seemed impressed with my gear, but I had made it seem too easy. I flipped it out there again, and caught another, smaller Nile perch. Then each of them gave it a try with no luck.

So I caught about six pounds of fish in five minutes, while they worked for an hour to catch one half-pound fish. I gave the men my fish, but I remember feeling like I had just reinforced how easy my life was compared to their lives. I'm sure they didn't think twice about it though.

One of the men who was dewatering the puddle – on a
different day after a fire hunt

***

On one occasion Adama invited J. Anne and me to accompany him and his brothers on a half-day trip up the river. We arrived at their little hamlet at first light, as instructed, only to find that they had already departed.

The women explained that the men had left early, but would be back for us very soon. That was the polite Malian way of saying that we were out of luck. We hung out for about an hour before we figured this out. So we eventually did the polite thing and said we'd "be back soon".

I was a little bit ticked off, but J. Anne and I were going fishing anyway, so it wasn't that bad.

We went to the "Old Man" hole and I caught a couple of Nile perch right away. Nile perch fishing (for small ones) is so much like largemouth bass fishing that I pretended we were fishing in a bass tournament against the guys who had ditched us. Then I caught a nice "kicker" of about five pounds and J. Anne added another nice one to give us a pretty decent five-fish bass tournament limit. (See the picture below with the binoculars around my neck.)

We went back to the fishing hamlet and hung out for a little while to see if the guys would show up. They did, and we compared catches. J. Anne and I won the first ever unsanctioned bass-fishing-for-Nile-perch tournament in the history of West Africa, probably.

I wondered whether these guys would resent me for taking fish that they might be able to catch and sell. But they didn't seem to mind. I had tried to explain my self-serving idea about men in the village buying fish instead of cigarettes, so maybe they thought my fishing was to their ultimate fish-selling benefit. I suspect though that they were just nice and generous. Plus, J. Anne and I were obviously pretty entertaining at times…

Coulda won a bass tournament...

***

Just about every Peace Corps volunteer I know had a kid or kids that hung around and made themselves indispensable. It took me a couple of months to warm up to Bougari and Tiékoro. But those guys turned out to be awesome. Bougari's village nickname was Village Chief, and he was obviously the top junior in the village. And Tiékoro was number two. I hadn't been aware

33

of it, but there was a clear social hierarchy that determined which kids were going to adopt the Americans.

Those two guys turned out to be the best cultural guides we had, and they were as funny to us as we were to them. Plus they brought our water to us every morning and always brought me any interesting insects they found. And since I had been given a Malian name – Yacouba – they suggested that I give them American names. So they became Steve and Jacko.

Most of my fishing trips were welcome escapes from unwanted attention in the village, so I usually snuck away when Steve and Jacko were not around. But one morning they made me take them. We went to my best hole before sunrise.

The two of them crossed the river and watched from the high cut bank. This was when the river was at its absolute minimum flow, and the Nile perch were stacked up right below the drop-off. It was probably three feet deep at the top of the cut, and maybe twice that in the hole. It was too deep to see the fish, but I could see right where the drop was. I yelled over to those guys and they said they couldn't see fish from up above either.

I cast a jig-head and grub right at the edge of the drop so that the lure would "tumble" in like drifting prey. I hooked up with what was easily the biggest fish I'd ever hooked. It was probably a good sized Nile perch, and even though it didn't break my line, it bent my too-small wire hook and pulled off.

Steve and Jocko were much less excited than I was. They never saw the fish and they had no point of reference for how much of a fight it had put up before it got away. That skinny little rod bent a lot – so what?

I spread my arms and said "*BELE-BELE!*" and they thought I was being funny, I guess.

Unlike tigerfish, Nile perch don't get all spooked when

34

one of their own gets hooked and thrashes around a bit. So I tied on another jig. I made the same cast and got bit right away. This time it was a fish I could handle though.

Steve and Jocko were excited now. I told them that this was a small one compared to the first one, but they gave me the "*BELE-BELE*" back like it was a huge one.

"This is a small one!"

"No, it's a big one! Do it again!"

I think I took a couple of casts before hooking up again. This one was a little bit bigger, and the guys were yelling for more.

But I said it was time to go. They couldn't believe it. They wanted to know whether I could catch more fish right then, and if so, why not? I just said that it was all we needed – one fish for us and one for a pregnant woman of their choice. The other fish could stay fresh in the river until tomorrow. They weren't so sure about that particular ethic.

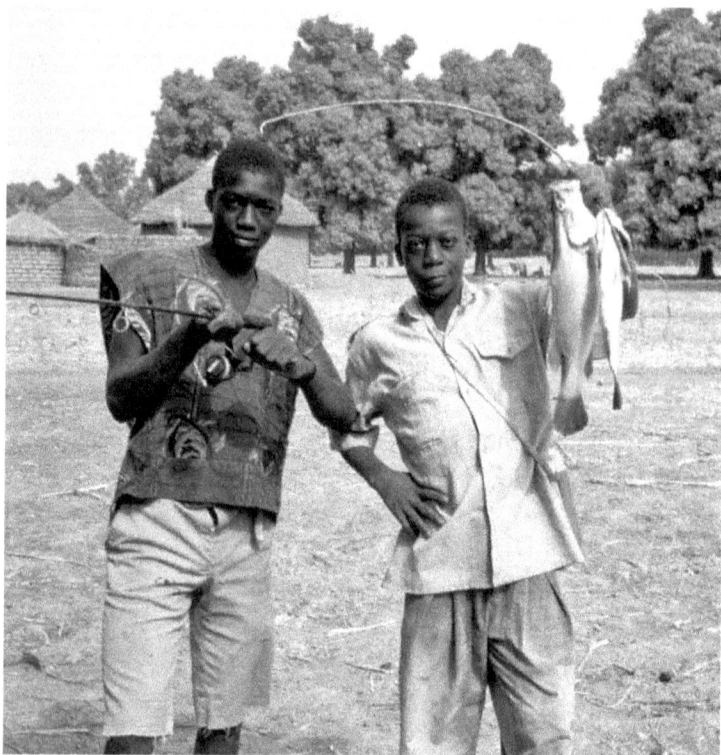

Steve (left) and Jocko wondering why we stopped at two

***

I ended up having my hooks bend three or four more times in that hole in the coming days. The biggest Nile perch I landed was the one in the picture at the start of this section. I'm calling it 10 pounds, but you can make up your own mind. I'm guessing that the ones I lost were twice that big and more. With heavier gear and forged hooks instead of wire, that spot would have impressed the hell out of Steve and Jocko.

And on what ended up being my last trip to that hole, I

thought I had been given another chance at landing a big one.

I had a bite on one of the grubs and hooked something very heavy. You've probably already guessed, right? Yeah, it was a *dodo* the size of a basketball! It was the biggest one I ever saw and I had it hooked by the tail. It was worth it for the laugh. I wish I had a picture of it all blown up.

That *dodo* ended up being the last fish I caught from the river at my village. However, I still had some time to fish in Bamako on my way out of the country. And the river runs through it too…

Earlier in the year some friends and I had caught a few tigerfish at a deep spot downstream from the submersible bridge at the end of town. It was a few miles from the Peace Corps hostel, but it was an easy-enough bike ride as long as you didn't get hit by a car.

The trouble with that spot is even though it is fairly big water, there were only two good places to cast from, and like I mentioned before, once you catch a tigerfish, the fishing hole shuts down. So our trips out there usually consisted of a half-hour bike ride, five minutes of tigerfish action, and a half-hour ride home.

The river below the submersible bridge was super deep. I couldn't even get a jig to the bottom. It was effectively bottomless, like we were standing on top of a high sandstone cliff with water flooded to its very top. It was a free flowing river there – not a reservoir or anything. It seems like it would be a good spot for an episode of River Monsters. I bet there's some HAWG Nile perch in that hole. Three-hundred pounds, anyone? BIG catfish? Well, I certainly don't know, but…

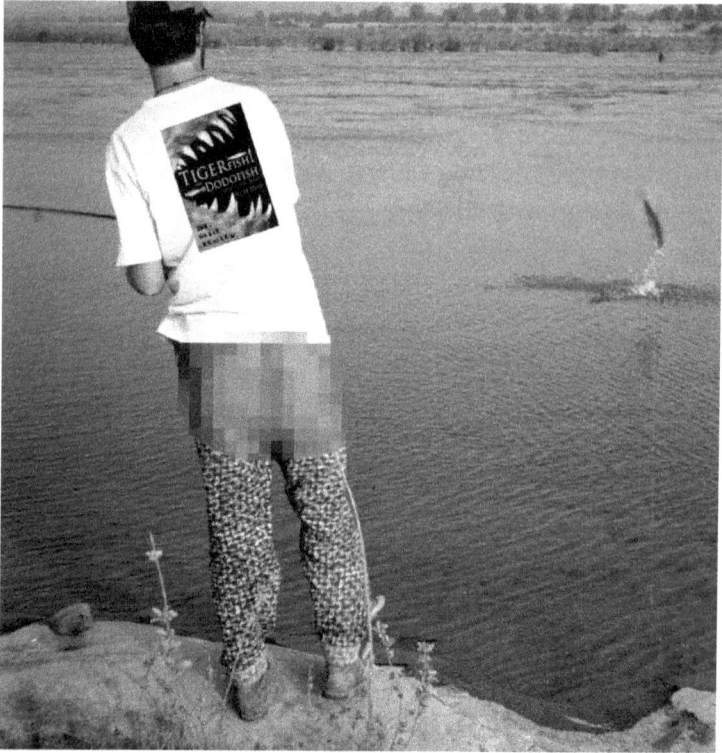

Tigerfish in Bamako. You can see where the "cliff" drops off out in front of me.   T-shirt altered and butt pixelated for obvious reasons.

***

Anyway, it was no problem getting tigerfish to bite a lure. It's not like you have to match the hatch and land a nymph right in front of the fish's face or anything. Just throw something out there and reel it in.

For me, the great challenge of tigerfishing was hooking them. Their heads are so bony and their teeth grip the lure so

38

hard, that you can't set the hook on them. They just grip the lure until they decide to let it go. There were times at my village when I could watch every little tigerfish in a school – twenty or more – take a turn biting my grub until they had all tasted it and stopped biting. And, of course, they were pretty good at simply cutting the line. Easy biting, difficult landing...

But once you actually hook one, they seem to get kind of pissed off.

I only caught more than one tigerfish at the submersible bridge on one occasion – my last trip out there. On that day I got to the main spot and cast a jig about as far as I could. I reeled it in quickly just under the surface. Maybe ten cranks into the retrieve I got slammed. This was the biggest tigerfish I would hook – six or eight pounds, perhaps. It jumped and jumped again and probably jumped again. And the line just went 'pink'. And that was that. I took a few casts, changed lures, and took a few more casts – nothing.

So I went over to the second casting spot closer to the bridge, which wasn't nearly as good a spot as the first spot. But I hooked up there right away too. This fish didn't jump and it was very strong. I wondered if it might be something other than a tigerfish. It turned out that I had hooked it in the back, right behind the dorsal fin.

The nice thing about hooking it in the back was that the lure was far from the teeth! It wasn't a big tigerfish, but a three pounder on my light gear was about all the fight I needed. I landed it without a problem though.

I took a few more casts in that spot and, of course, got nothing. So we went birdwatching and insect collecting for a while to give the first spot a chance to recover.

I eventually went back to the first spot and threw the same chartreuse-sparkle curly-tail plastic grub out there and got one to bite without hooking itself. It let go of the lure and another one bit briefly before spitting the lure, and then I finally hooked the third one that bit – all on the same cast. This fish jumped a bunch of times and just as I tried to pull it up on the shallow rock slab in front of me, the line broke. I only hurt myself a little bit diving for it.

I was able to grab the fish by the tail, and according to my Peace Corps friend Greg, I punched the fish in the head until it succumbed. I was pretty excited, I guess, and I don't recall the punching part very clearly. But it wouldn't be the first time I had punched a fish in the head, so, yeah, it probably went down that way.

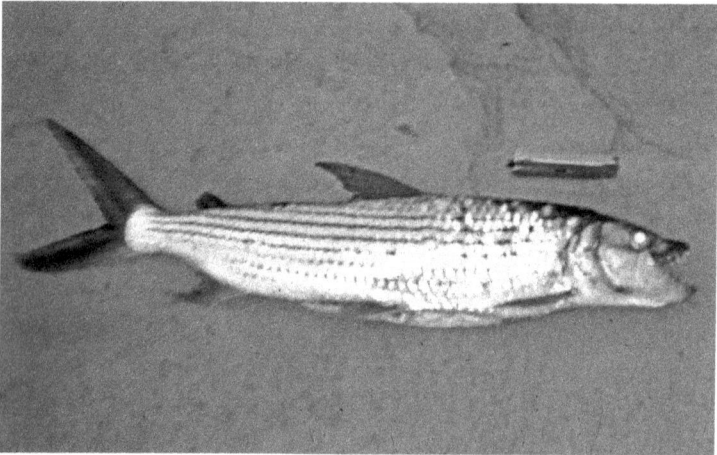

Blurry tigerfish, punched in the head. (Hopefully this is the worst picture you will ever see in a book that isn't about Bigfoot or the Loch Ness Monster.)

***

Anyway, this was the biggest tigerfish I landed. It was about twenty-two inches long and weighed maybe five pounds. (It's also the one jumping in the picture above.)

I kept these fish to give to the guard back at the hostel. Then on the ride home the smaller of the two fish came loose from my bike rack and got wedged between the rack and the spokes. I almost fell into traffic. Dembelé the guard seemed pleased with the fish despite the scuff marks.

When I returned to Mali in 2005 I fished three times at my village and – I'll make this short – I got skunked.

And my friend Diallo, a cattle herder, also getting skunked

***

COMMUNITY FISHING EVENTS

This region of Mali is best known for being the 13th Century home of the great warrior king Mansa Sundiata Keita of the Mandé Empire and his famous griot singers – who are still singing and reciting the history today. Then if you don't count gold mining, growing peanuts, and smuggling untaxed cigarettes from Guinea; the region might be next best known for these big community fishing events.

A large community fishing event on a floodplain lake

***

There are dozens of floodplain lakes and ponds of varying sizes in this area. So there are dozens of community fishing events of varying sizes as well. Some, like the one above on a large lake, can include thousands of people. Other events are organized by smaller civic groups, like the village women's cooperative pictured below.

And a small one on a dammed tributary stream

***

And there was even an annual event on a pond set aside for the children of my village. The kids' pond wasn't the biggest or most productive, but as you can see in the pictures below, the kids got 'em!

A pond set aside for children. (That's Jacko in the red.)

***

Kids catch fish too!

***

These fishing events occur late in the hottest part of the dry season – from March to May. The larger events are scheduled by a "pond master" (*dalatigi*) based on the water levels. So the exact timing may vary by several weeks between years. They are primarily waiting until the water is shallow enough for people to be able to wade the deepest parts.

And NOBODY is allowed to fish in these ponds that year before the pond master says it's time to fish. This allows the fish to finish spawning and hatching unmolested. Even on the day of the event, everyone has to wait until the pond master tells a blacksmith to give the signal by being first in the water. In the picture below, everyone is waiting in the heat and getting very impatient. They are looking for the signal to come from the place where you can see a small puff of smoke by the trees through the blue net.

Hey, you two guys should be watching the smoke.

***

The event pictured above and below was the largest one I saw. I estimated that there were about three-thousand people surrounding the water waiting and waiting... People had come from many miles around – some walking all day – and now they were complaining that the pond master was on an ego trip. But once the blacksmith gave the signal, they knew what to do.

Circling the fish

***

People with the small triangular nets formed a series of circles and slowly closed in on the fish. It gets exciting when the fish panic. Larger fish, especially tigerfish and moonfish, sometimes jump clear out of the circle over someone's head.

The people with the conical trap baskets moved around on the outside of the circles. And men with spears worked the aquatic vegetation around the edge of the pond. (There's a link to my video of two of the smaller events in the appendices.)

Before going into more detail about gear and management, here's some of what they catch:

Big knifefish

***

The fish above is *Gymnarchus niloticus*, or African knifefish. It has very small eyes and produces electricity that may help it sense its environment in the dense vegetation where it is often found. Their meat is a little rubbery and reminded me of scallops, so they were pretty good eating. This is one of the bigger ones I saw.

(By the way, I've obscured the man's face because I don't know his name or where he came from, and I was unable to get permission to use his image. Recognizable faces are people I know who have given me permission me to use their images for "the project" I told them I was hoping to work on. This publication is that project. A lot of the people gave permission on the condition that they get a copy of the photo, and prints have been presented to everyone. And any of the scant royalties I expect to receive will offset the annual contributions that J. Anne and I make to help support a teacher and a health worker in the village.)

Nile perch, child's foot, Madame Kouyaté
***

Very big moonfish

***

The fish above is the largest *Citharhinus* (moonfish) that I saw, by far. And if I hadn't obscured the man's face, you could see that he seemed pleased about it too. This fish is in the same order (Characiformes) as piranhas and tigerfish, but without the impressive teeth.

Being careful with a tigerfish – using a metal rod to knock out teeth

***

Tigerfish are called *wulujege* in Malinké, which means "dogfish". There are at least three species of tigerfish in Mali, but locals didn't distinguish between them as far as I could tell. And I can't be sure from the pictures which are which. Anyway, they don't get nearly as large as the famous Goliath tigerfish of East Africa. The one in the picture above is about as big as I saw.

53

Like a lot of fish, including sharks, tigerfish have replacement teeth that move into place when an older tooth is lost. Tigerfish are supposedly mainly fish eaters, but I've heard that they will attack other small animals, such as aquatic birds. However, they are wary and don't seem to present a hazard to swimmers or waders.

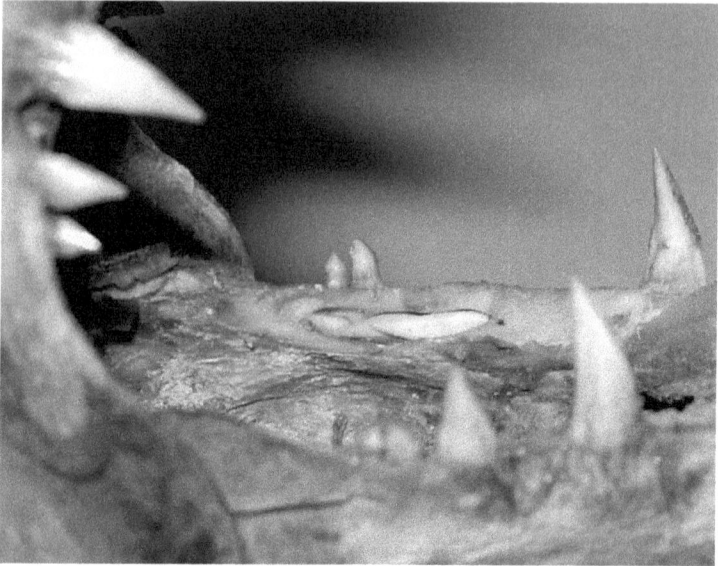

Tigerfish skull showing replacement teeth down in the jaw

***

More about the gear used in these events:

The stick baskets, called *sousou*, are surprisingly effective. They have a small opening at the top, so when they are dropped down over a fish you can reach in and grab it. They are mainly used by women who wade along, shove the basket down, then pick it up and take a couple of steps before pushing it down again. When they feel a fish freaking out inside, they reach in from the top and grab it.

On the way to a fishing event with *sousou* basket traps

***

A *sousou* demonstration

***

The most common fishing implement is a small stick-framed triangular net – used either singly or in pairs. Locally they are called *jo*, which is simply "net". I've seen them in the literature called "clap nets" too – presumably because you can clap them together to secure a fish. Like the man below has done…

Clapping the clap nets around a fish

***

And when Modibo strikes a dramatic pose with his *jo*, you use his picture...

***

Men also use pairs of spears, called *masakaw*, that are made from a sharpened piece of iron re-bar with a wooden handle attached. The men walk along through the aquatic vegetation alternately stabbing with each spear as they go. I noticed that they didn't usually stab the fish outright. They normally stabbed close enough to the fish to find out where it was first, and then were able to stab it. The fish were usually unable to get away due to the dense vegetation.

In the picture below, there is a fish in the midst of the crowd, and the younger guys are giving deference to the old man as he stabs around for it. However, if the fish starts to get away, the other guys will make an effort.

I wouldn't want to be the fish in there…

***

Sometimes the vegetation is so thick that you'd swear there was no water under it. However, knifefish, African lungfish, *Bichir*, and walking catfish are air breathers that don't need a whole lot of water.

And if you are wondering whether this spearing technique is dangerous…

Burulai with some lungfish

TIGERFISH!

***

This is my friend Burulai. He has a few lungfish, and I think that's a *Bichir* (pronounced "biker") at left, and perhaps a small walking catfish too. A week later Burulai was stabbed in the side of the toe by a careless boy at another fishing event. Luckily, he did not get a bad infection. He said he wasn't mad at the boy, but his explanation for why he wasn't mad left me believing that perhaps he had once stabbed someone himself.

One of the pond masters said something about bichirs that I wrote down as "he alerts other fish first". I think he meant that the bichirs alert the other fish to the presence of people.

Like many of the other fish in this water, bichirs (also called ropefish and snake fish) have to breathe air, so they live close to the surface in shallow water near the edge of a pond. I once had a male bichir in an aquarium, and he was very alert and quick moving, even though it didn't look like he would be. So it wouldn't surprise me if bichirs at the surface in the weeds react like frogs and jump away when someone approaches. I never noticed it myself – or maybe I thought they really WERE frogs.

Big walking catfish

***

The large fish above is the biggest walking catfish I saw. As their name implies, these fish can move across land to find better habitat if, for example, their pond is drying up. They have become an invasive pest species in places like the Florida Everglades. They were one of the more common fish captured by spear, and they seemed to be the most common larger fish found in local sauce and rice dishes.

The catfish below looks similar to the walking catfish

above, but it is in the genus *Heterobranchus* rather than *Clarias*. They are both air-breathing catfish, but *Clarias* is the true walking catfish.

More remarkable than these catfish, perhaps, is the Dogon hat worn by my blacksmith friend Camara. Camara is not Dogon (the ethnic group that is from the cliff region in central Mali). However, he explained that Mandé blacksmiths and Dogon blacksmiths are "like brothers" and will share each other's customs as a sign of that connection. Camara is the blacksmith who signaled the start of this fishing event, but he did not fish.

Heterobranchus catfish and Camara the blacksmith in his
Dogon hat

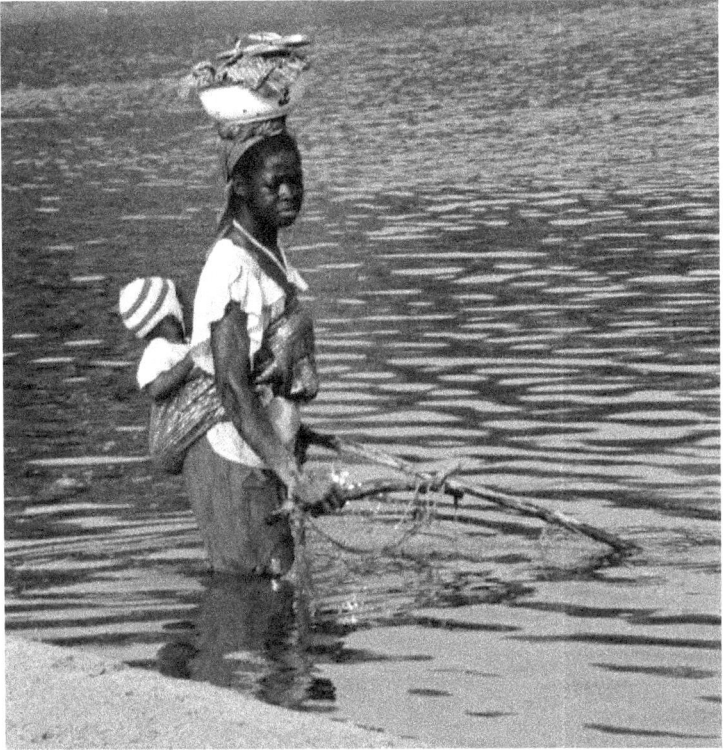

Fishing with a large A-frame net

***

Another type of net used primarily by women is a large A-frame like the one above. The way the women are able to balance everything while landing fish and being a mother is an amazing thing to observe. The kids always seemed to enjoy the ride – splashing the water or snoozing.

Okay – back to the rules and regulations.

As mentioned before, the pond master calls the shots. Each pond master has inherited his position from a long line of pond masters in his family. Each village that has domain over ponds usually has a pond master. However, the biggest ponds in my area belonged to one village, but their pond master was from a different village that didn't have ponds of its own. The reasons for this arrangement were complicated and had happened so many generations before that no one was exactly sure why it was that way. (Or perhaps they just didn't want to tell me why…)

The pond masters said they will schedule up to four community fishing events per pond per season – or possibly none at all if the water never drops enough. Everyone is allowed to fish the biggest events, no matter who they are or how far away they live. But no one is allowed to fish during that season until the pond master says so.

I asked what would happen if they caught someone fishing out of season. They said the person would be fined and have their gear confiscated, and that a severe beating wouldn't be out of the question. They also implied that there were certain "spiritual consequences" as well. But, as usual, they weren't interested in detailing what the spiritual consequences might be. Anyway, none of them was aware of anyone ever fishing out of season, so any consequences remained to be seen.

One spiritual consequence that, for some reason, they were willing to talk about involved a large white horse that was supposed to live at the bottom of the river. This horse was responsible for changes in the course of the river channel. If a village was disrespectful of the river, this horse was able to move the river farther away from the village. This was widely known to have happened to a village just upstream from ours due to some sort of pollution issue.

Anyway, individual people are also allowed to fish in the ponds after all of the scheduled fishing events are finished. But other than a few kids digging lungfish from dried-up areas, I didn't see anyone fishing the ponds after the big events.

Most of the larger fishing events are held on Mondays, which is called "The Devil's Day" for some reason. The Devil is said to own the gold in the river, so out of respect the people don't pan for gold on Mondays, which gives them time for fishing and hunting.

And there are particular ponds that are only fished on Tuesdays or Wednesdays. I believe the reason for this was simply to schedule a few consecutive fishing days for people who may have come from out of the area. The picture below is of an event in one of the Tuesday/Wednesday ponds.

A Tuesday/Wednesday event

***

The big Monday events are preceded by special ceremonies that begin on the Sunday and last into the next afternoon. I don't know about elsewhere along the river, but in my area the pond masters and their associates did sixteen hours of drumming and dancing, plus certain "secret activities" that were performed by blacksmiths.

In the picture a few pages up, the puff of blue smoke is from the fire where the ceremonies were taking place. I'm not sure what else the ceremonies are supposed to accomplish, but they are probably a good way to scare off any dangerous animals before the crowd arrives, if nothing else.

I also asked the pond masters if farmers and herders were allowed to use the ponds. They said that animals were allowed to drink, but that the herders tended to keep the cows moving so they didn't completely trample the habitat. They also said that farmers could draw water for irrigation if they got permission from the pond master.

From what I could see, irrigation and cattle watering were not significant habitat degraders in most of the bigger ponds and wetlands. Some of the ponds seemed to have regular cattle use, however – like below.

Spearing in the shallows

***

I also asked what they thought about the efficiency of their fish harvest methods – whether the various techniques might be too efficient, or not efficient enough. They said they liked it the way it was, and added that they wouldn't want more efficiency as some fish need to get away for the future. I guess that a thousand years of sustainable fisheries is all the evidence anyone needs.

I should say that the Malian federal government manages

the sport and commercial fisheries, and other river uses in cooperation with the other nations in the Niger River watershed. But the local pond-master-style of management of the community fishing events is officially left to people at the village level. "Decentralized management" is the bureaucratic term for it.

I also asked the pond masters if there had ever been any large fish die-offs in the lakes or smaller ponds. They said no – they had never heard of any fish kills on the floodplain or in the river.

BUT… And this is true… On the first morning of my return in 2005, it rained the hardest and longest that I had seen in almost two and a half years of living in Mali. The area's agricultural extension agent told me that it had rained 3.25 inches in under two hours. And there had been a fish kill.

It was Early March – right in the thick of the hot-dry season – so this rain was a freak event. Supposedly, ashes from recently burned fields washed into a major tributary during the storm and a bunch of Nile perch died. This tributary was *Le Fié* – where I'd been shocked by the elephantfish in 1993.

Lasine Sogoré getting skunked on *Le Fié* a few days after the fish kill in 2005

***

Our long-time friend Namissakoro with a decent haul from a small pond in 2005

***

It looks like Namissakoro had a few small moonfish, a couple of *Bagrus* catfish, some cichlids, a bonytongue, maybe a small tigerfish, and another catfish that I can't make out.

***

A small African bonytongue

***

Clap nets

***

A small Nile perch, an African bonytongue, a *Tilapia*, an elephantfish, and a nice walking catfish taken by clap net

***

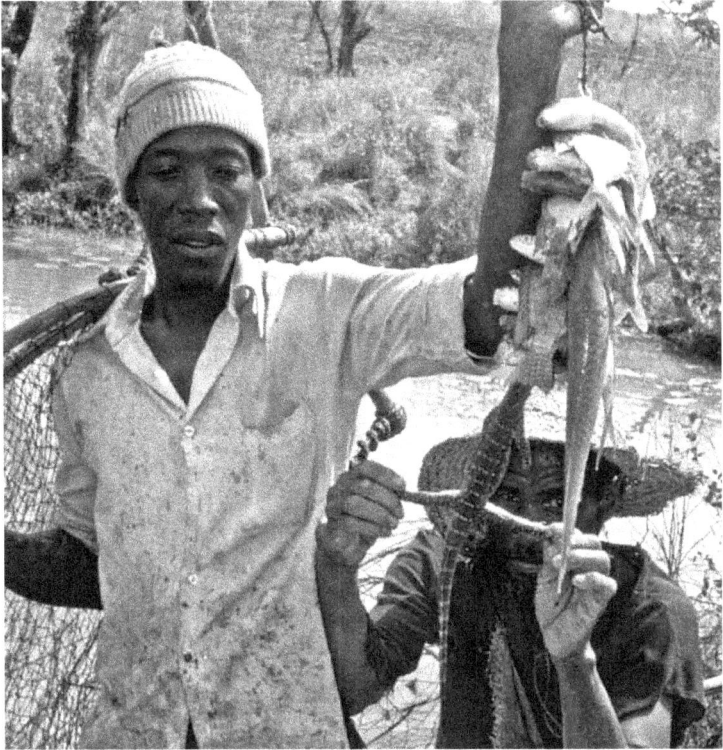

The Cissé brothers with a small Nile monitor lizard and the usual assortment of fish. The man in the straw hat was a super nice guy who had a permanently dislocated right wrist. His handshake was fine though…

***

A nice *Tilapia*…

***

Here's a small event (above) in one of my village's ponds.

***

The long walk to the fishing grounds... The mushroom-
shaped objects are termite mounds.

***

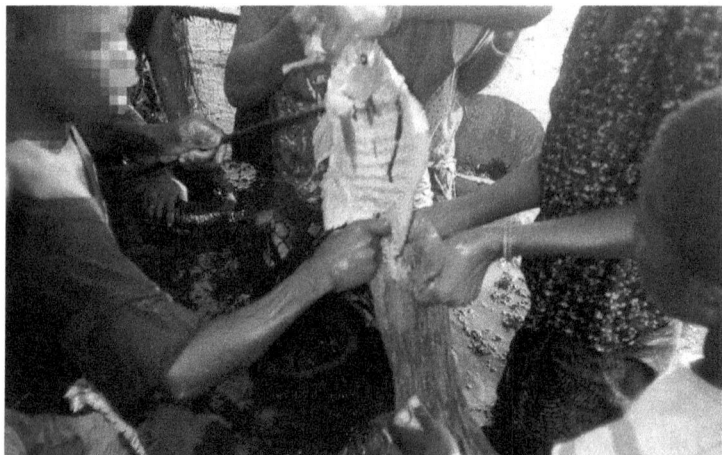

Another nice *Tilapia*

***

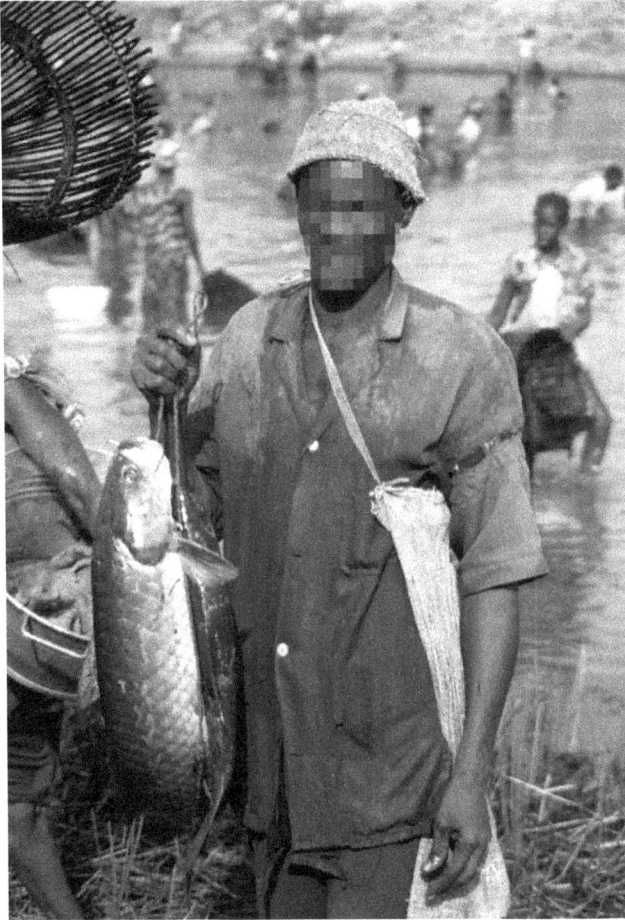

This gentleman has a couple of *Heterotis niloticus* (aka African bonytongue or African arowana). The band around his upper arm is a fetish that is for protection from snakes – or at least that's what I was told. But you can never be too sure about these things…

***

A couple of successful brothers

***

Here's my friend "Jacko" (above, left) and his brother with a couple of knifefish and a bonytongue. Jacko was pretty dang proud of himself for catching that fish. Most people can't afford to buy fish like this very often, so the days of the big events are feast days. The pond masters confirmed what I had already figured out for myself – Nile perch is the best and the knifefish is second best to eat. I expressed my opinion that *Tilapia* and other cichlids could be third, and they said that the cichlids are "healthy for old people". And everyone likes catfish too.

The pond before the storm

***

Above is a shot of what some of the ponds look like before all those people rush in. Like I said before, the ponds don't seem to suffer long-term damage. Of course, we don't know what it was like here before people – when this place was probably loaded with herds of big animals using the ponds.

African rock python

***

The snake above is an African rock python. The guy in the background is laughing because there's a woman standing behind me berating the man in the white hat for wanting to eat the snake. The man was defending himself – essentially saying that the woman was an ignorant hick for wanting to kill the snake and then wasting all that perfectly good meat. Apparently, the woman was arguing about some kind of snake magic that was gonna get the guy if he ate it.

Cane rat

***

The above animal is a large rodent called a grasscutter or cane rat. They are common in that area and are occasionally caught during the fishing events. The meat is very tender. These animals are also raised for their meat in some places in West Africa.

Downstream end of a dam trap

***

Another kind of artisanal fishing method involved the use of static traps and fish dams. The picture above is the downstream side of a funnel trap weir at the mouth of a small seasonal drainage. The picture below is the upstream side on another one. Unfortunately, I never saw anyone building or working these dams. I think they tended them when the river was still too high for me to go slogging around out there.

Upstream side of a dam trap

***

The trap below is a passive/submerged trap that had a small catfish in it. I don't think they need to bait this kind of trap – the fish just find their way in as they forage, and then can't find their way back out of the funnel-shaped entrance.

Funnel trap

***

COMMERCIAL FISHING

When I wasn't helping J. Anne with a health lesson, playing foosball with my teachers, fishing at the river, hanging out at the blacksmith forge, or bird watching and bug collecting, I could probably be found with the Somono fishermen. (Adama and the guys who ditched me before the Nile perch "tournament"…)

One thing I can tell you for sure about Somono fishers is that they don't like dodos.

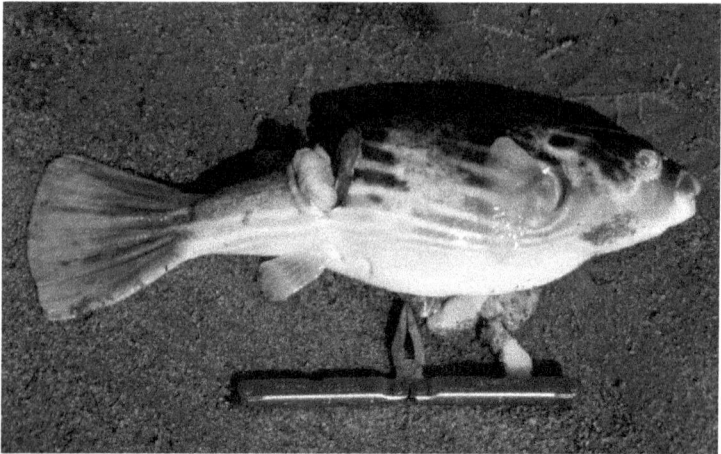

A dead *dodo*

***

The commercial fishermen always kill dodos if they catch them – due to their habit of biting through nets. I found the one in the picture above – chopped with a machete and left on the riverbank. The tool in the picture is seven inches long, so that

86

dodo would blow up to about the size of a volleyball. I was told that the guts were good for killing cats and that this was the dodo's only use.

Another thing that the fishers don't like is cobras – probably for obvious reasons. I was with Adama and his friends one time and we saw a cobra swimming right toward the boat. The snake looked like it knew what it was doing. It must have thought we were a log.

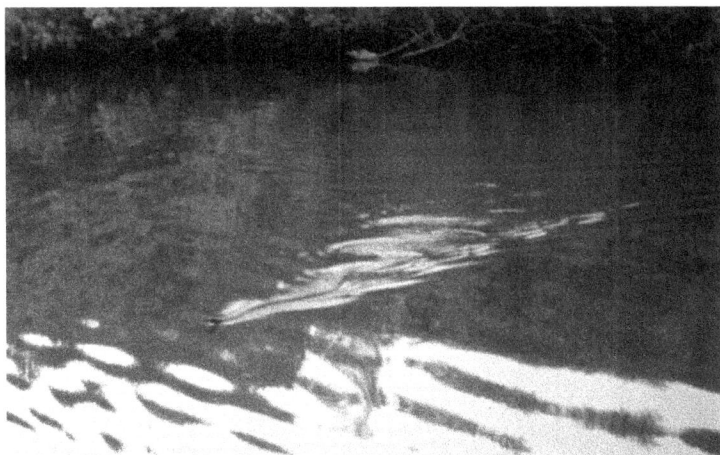

A cobra swimming in the wrong direction

***

The cobra swam right up to them, and the guys beat the crap out of it with the push pole. Then they posed for a picture and tossed it as far as they could by using the pole as a catapult. I thought they might at least keep it for the skin. And I would have liked to examine it. But, no, that thing was not welcome in the boat dead or alive.

What happens when cobras swim in the wrong direction

***

On another occasion, I was visiting a family in a temporary fishing camp on a sand bar. A cobra happened to go crawling by. It was actually crawling in the right direction, but too close and not fast enough. The man I was speaking with grabbed his shotgun, shot the cobra twice, beat it with a canoe push pole, posed for a picture, and catapulted the snake far out into the river. The two shotgun shells were a considerable expense – but expense must be measured against how much you hate cobras, I guess.

Another ex-cobra

***

The Somono fishermen aren't exactly an ethnic group. They are considered to be more of an occupational class of people, though they obviously have a cultural identity and history. They are a separate group from the more well-known Bozo fishermen from farther downstream in central Mali.

The Somonos' fishing techniques include a variety of set

lines with single or multiple hooks, passive fish traps, cast nets, A-frame nets, and monofilament gill nets. The Somonos in my area lived both in small villages or "hamlets" near the river, and in temporary camps on the sandbars when the river was low.

Somono family with tigerfish and a *Bagrus* catfish

***

A Somono fishing camp about to get a visit from some cows

***

My main fisher friends, the Sogoré family, invited me along during one of their multi-family fishing get-togethers. The other migrating Somono families had reached our part of the river, and my friends were the local hosts.

There were about a dozen families participating, and I had never met most of the people. So we shared a lot of greetings and fishing benedictions, which was a fun way to get in some language practice.

The different groups, each in their own canoe, set their own gillnets. They secured the nets between the sandbar and the riparian trees on the deep side of a secondary channel near the confluence with *Le Fié*. The nets were weighted at the bottom with terra cotta weights or rocks.

Fishermen from elsewhere on the river

***

Adama and brothers prepping their gillnets

***

Adama diving for net weight rocks

***

Gillnet deployment

***

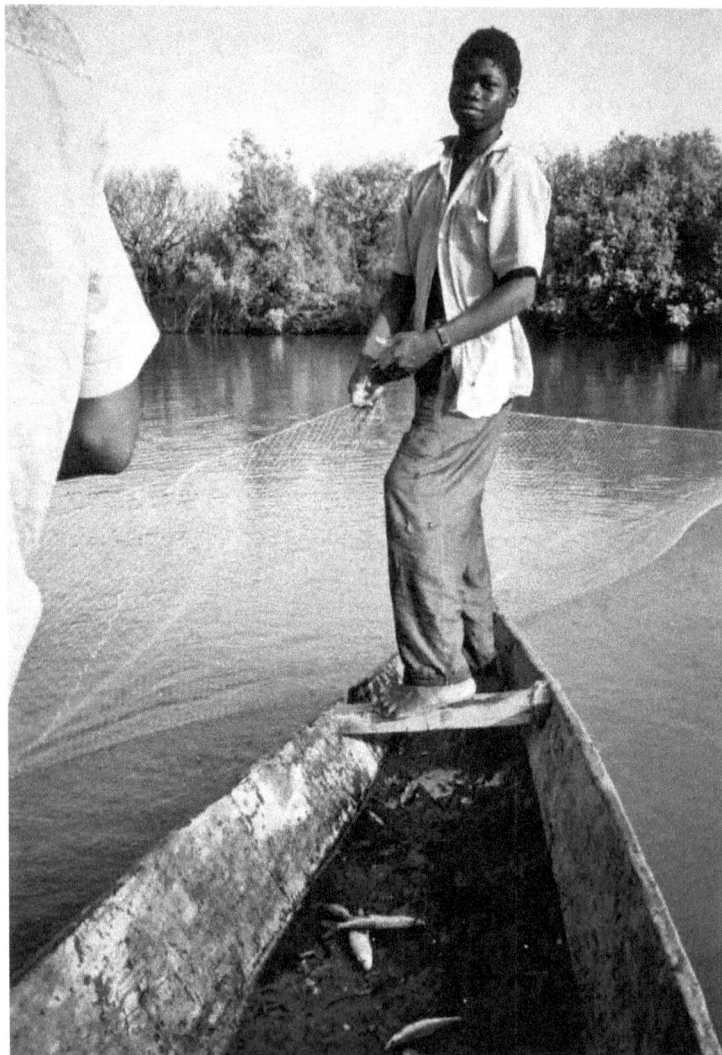

Tending the net and removing small fish

***

Adama removing a Nile perch from his gillnet

***

Gillnetted bonytongues and a *Tilapia* (FYI: The map on the Micro Machines shirt is of Saskatchewan, Canada)

***

Once the nets were set, the fishermen pushed their canoes back and forth and removed fish as they went. They caught mostly small fish. The biggest fish that I saw that day were the Nile perch that Adama is pulling in, and the two bonytongues that the boys are holding in the pictures above.

I never saw them catch a really big Nile perch, but one morning I saw a fisherman wading down the river holding a rope.

I greeted him and he came over to show me what he had. He was towing a live Nile perch that looked to be about fifty pounds. He was keeping it alive in the water so it would still be fresh when he got to market. He must have had about twelve miles to go if I understood his plan. At least he was going downstream…

The biggest Nile perch I saw was an easy hundred-pounder at a market in Bamako. On another occasion I saw a guy walking in a town I happened to be travelling through who was carrying a huge Nile perch head. I asked him if I could take this picture. He was happy to oblige, but unfortunately I was not able to give him a copy of the photo.

Using some fisheries data, I determined the approximate length of the fish based on an estimate of the head length, then I converted that to known length/weight relationships for Nile perch. The fish was possibly 150 centimeters (five feet) long, which would put it well over one-hundred pounds. Just an educated guess, but that's a heck of fish head no matter how you view it…

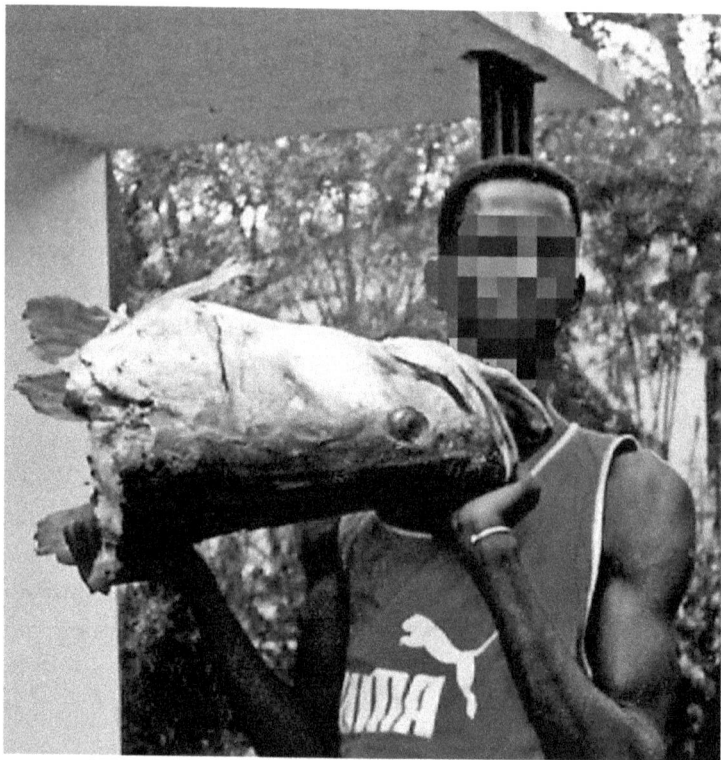

Nile perch head

***

When I went back to Mali in 2005, I was very happy to find the same fishing families in the same places where I had last seen them eleven years before. My best fisherman friend Adama had left, but his younger brother Lasine, who had been a little boy the last time I saw him (and was not responsible for ditching me that one time) seemed happy to take me out on the river on short notice. We fished with the rod and reel that I'd brought, but like I said, we caught zip. It was a great boat trip though, and

I got to visit artisanal gold miners from my village, and shoot a bunch of video.

When we left Mali in 1994, I gave my rod and tackle to Adama. I was hoping to find out whether he had ever caught anything with it – even a *dodo*. Unfortunately, no one knew the answer.

The Somono patriarch whose name I can't remember, 2005

***

I also got a chance to see Lasine make the lead weights for a cast net. You can see in the pictures how he pokes a hole in the sand with a dowel for a mold, and then makes the weight's hole by inserting a straw before pouring the molten lead. Pretty nifty!

Lasine making cast-net weights

***

I was happy to see Adama's and Lasine's father, Sékou Sogoré, again too. That's him with the shotgun and cowboy hat.

Sékou was going blind from the "river blindness" disease – like so many of the old people on the river. There was even an entire village up *Le Fié* that had been abandoned due to river blindness. The disease is transmitted via the bite of a blackfly – a tiny little bastard with tiny littler bastards living in it, with yet tinier little bastards living in them. And then within those tiny bastards there are bacteria that apparently cause an immune system reaction that causes the blindness. The actual name of the disease is onchocerciasis.

Sékou Sogoré posing with his local blacksmith-made shotgun in 2005.

***

Sekou Sogoré and family in 2005.

***

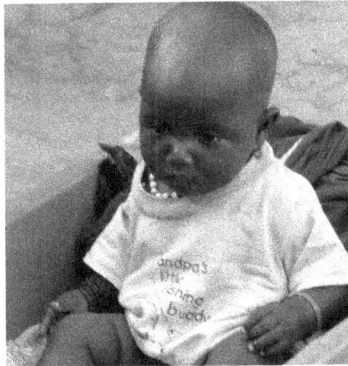

The family knew that the t-shirt was made for a fishing family's kid, but they didn't know what it said. They seemed delighted to find out – at least more delighted than the little girl was in having her picture taken...

TIGERFISH!

***

My favorite single communication experience in Mali came thanks to an old blind man. There was a big fishing event scheduled for the Monday before our final departure from our village. I was riding there on my bike on an unfamiliar trail and I pulled up to a hamlet of six or eight huts. I stopped to get directions and found that everyone but a blind man and a little girl had gone fishing.

The man was seated in the center of the family compound. The girl – who was maybe eight years old – hid behind the man. I greeted the man, and the little girl kept quiet. After a string of greetings and benedictions – that I had become proficient at by now – the man asked if I was from Ivory Coast.

At first it didn't occur to me that he thought I was an African. The little girl seemed pretty nervous, so I smiled at her put my finger to my lips. I answered "no" that I wasn't from Ivory Coast, and then he guessed Burkina Faso. The little girl couldn't hold it anymore and told him that I was a white man.

That's when I realized that he had mistaken me for an actual African. He said that my accent gave me away as a foreigner – but one who spoke a similar dialect, such as Bobo or Dioula. We had a big laugh together about that, and the little girl finally relaxed. He told the girl to show me the correct path to the fishing event. And I was on my way with a big smile on my face...

***

Okay – the following pictures are from one of the temporary fishing camps on the sandbar in 2005. The man in front of the family picture below is the man who shot the cobra in 1993. I'm ashamed that I can't remember his name. He was such a nice guy, and he really liked our book of West African birds. He is also the man throwing the cast net in the picture below, and polling the canoe above.

Somono family at sandbar fishing camp in 2005

***

Right before I took these pictures, Camara and Lasine showed me a small fish trap. There were a couple of catfish and a small cichlid in it. They told me that the cichlid was called *sambafagateben* which means "elephant-killing cichlid". (*Samba* is "elephant", *faga* is "kill", *teben* is the general name for cichlids including *Tilapia*.) Camara explained how this fish supposedly swims up an elephant's trunk when it's drinking, and the elephant beats its trunk on logs and rocks trying to dislodge it. The elephant eventually dies from its wounds and loss of its trunk. They haven't actually seen this happen themselves, but that's how it got its name. I'm pretty sure that it is a cichlid of the genus *Hemichromis*, or the African jewel cichlids.

Unfortunately, I did not take any still pictures of the trap or the fish. I shot some video though, and a link to the clip on YouTube is provided in the list of links at the end of this ebook.

Repairing a cast-net

***

Alestes in the same family as tigerfish – Charadidae

***

Another of the electric elephantfish family – Mormyridae

***

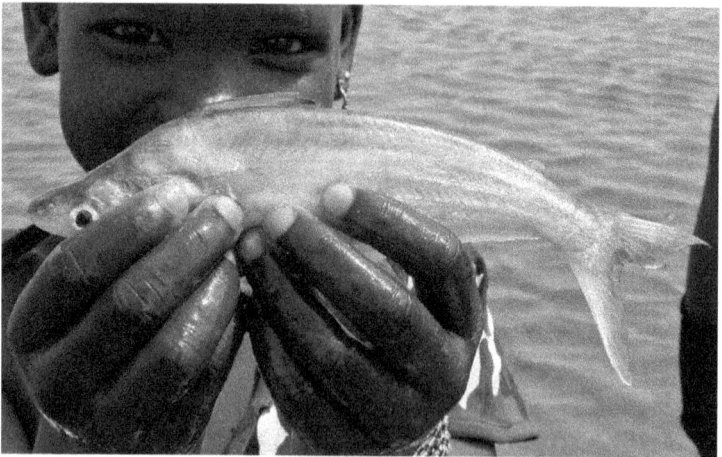

A catfish from the Schilbeidae family

***

These kids and I had a great time looking at their catch. I've always thought it must have been like having a clown come to your birthday party when I showed up. Some little kids were afraid of the pale galoot, but most kids were quick to laugh at any silliness – intentional, or otherwise.

Somono women and kids washing dishes and swimming – and ready to provide ferry service. (Just past the trees at right is where the Old Man Nile perch hole is.)

***

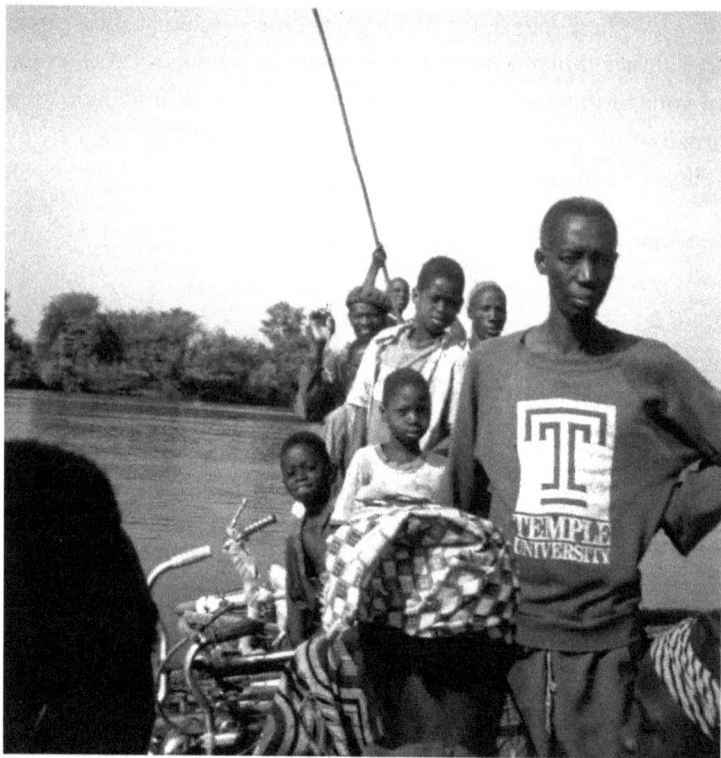

Catching the ferry in 1993 for my commute to two schools
across the river

***

J. Anne tried her hand at push polling. Here is Adama going back for the pole. I have to confess that I never tried it myself. I would have fallen out of the boat...

***

The Somono hamlet near my village in 1993. This is where we were ditched by Adama...

***

This cast caught a *Synodontis* up-side-down catfish

***

Somono women using A-frame nets on receding side
channel in 1993

***

Somono women on their way to market in 2005

***

Somono women at our Friday market in 1992 with some
Synodontis up-side-down catfish for sale in foreground

***

This is J. Anne's co-worker and all-around great guy, Tiékoura Diarra, with an elephantfish that we bought from the Somonos at our market in 1993.

***

At the beginning, I described my fear of hippos and crocs as an "imaginary" fear. It wasn't completely imaginary, but the larger dangerous animals were pretty rare on our reach of the river. I only saw one hippo within bike-riding distance of my village, and J. Anne saw the group of hippos in the picture above while on a trip with friends to Dogon Country. We did,

117

however, see hippo tracks near our village all the time. According to the Somonos, hippos lived up *Le Fié* and often came down to our area at night or in the rainy season. The picture below is of adult and juvenile tracks left in the bank after the river dropped.

***

Fire Hunts

The following section contains illustrated description of fire hunts that I witnessed while I was a Peace Corps volunteer in Mali, West Africa. These hunts took place in 1993 on the floodplain of the Niger River in southern Mali.

And if you have read my novel Used Aliens, this ebook serves to illustrate one of the major scenes. In the novel, aliens interfere with a fire hunt in a fictional Malian village. I have included an excerpt from Used Aliens at the end of this book.

***

The first section below depicts a fire hunt that was conducted mainly by young men and children, with only a couple of adult hunters with guns participating. The second section shows a fire hunt that was organized and conducted by older, established hunters. And the final few pictures illustrate additional points about the culture of Malian hunters.

These hunts typically took place on Mondays. Monday was known as The Devil's Day for some reason. The Devil supposedly owned the gold in the river, so out of respect the people did not mine gold on Mondays. Mondays are when they hunted and fished instead.

And I've taken the opportunity to say a few things about the hunter I knew best – the one pictured on the cover – Lasine Koné.

***

This is Lasine Koné with a small **Nile monitor** lizard at the start of the rainy season when everything (other than Lasine's jacket) starts to turn green again.

***

After a visit to my house for pictures, Lasine Koné leads the parade away. You can see him on the right under the mango tree bending over. He is standing in the back of a donkey cart dealing with a warthog and piglets that were tied up and not looking very comfortable in the pictures I took. So I didn't include them. The point of showing this picture is to show how everyone – not just the Americans – was fascinated by the animals and Lasine's hunting prowess.

***

This picture was from near the end of our Peace Corps service, and my wife's replacement volunteer was visiting our village for the very first time. Lasine had just butchered and sold this warthog, so he brought the head over for show-and-tell. The new volunteer was impressed, I think. And Lasine thought that he looked like a better runner than me...

***

ABOUT LASINE KONE

I knew Lasine while I was a Peace Corps volunteer in Mali, West Africa from 1992 to 1994. I returned to my village in 2005 and learned that he had been killed in a fall while hunting just one month before.

Early in my Peace Corps service I mentioned the name of my village to a taxi driver in the capital. He seemed surprised, and then he asked if I knew the "magic hunter".

There were a lot of hunters in my area, and they all seemed to practice divination and fetishism, but "magic hunter" didn't ring a bell. Then the man described a hunter who without a gun who could make animals leave the bush with him.

I said, "You mean Lasine Koné?"

"Yes!" was the taxi driver's enthusiastic answer. He seemed very impressed that I had been on a hunt with Lasine and had personally witnessed his so-called magic.

It turned out that Lasine was a minor celebrity. I even found a post card with a picture of him sitting on a huge dead crocodile. And he was especially well-known in expat circles for being able to deliver live warthogs.

Usually Lasine (and his dogs) would catch a warthog, pen it up, and then spread the word that one was available. The drivers of the morning bush taxis that ran between Bamako and Guinea would deliver the message to somebody in Bamako. And usually within a day or two a 4X4 pick-up would arrive to purchase the animal and Lasine's slaughter services.

Warthog is very good if you like pork. But a dead warthog is difficult to sell because few people in rural Mali – even non-Muslims – openly eat pork. Keeping it alive for the expats was where the money was. French expats love a fresh warthog barbeque. And Lasine was one of the few, if not the only one, who could reliably fill their orders for live ones.

Sometimes he'd get an advance commission for a warthog. Late one night he banged on my door asking if I'd give him a ride on my moped to the police station in the town about twelve miles up the road. Someone had told him that the police commandant was looking for a warthog and would be willing to take a hunter into the bush to find one.

Lasine was frantic to be the one who got there first. All he had to do was find the warthog and the commandant would shoot it – even though it was the middle of the night. Lasine explained that it was going to be easy money. So I may have broken a few Peace Corps rules, but I took him. And I woke up the next morning to find a warthog shoulder outside my front door.

The ironic thing about Lasine was that he was known as the "magic hunter" while being the only hunter who didn't use "magic". As far as I could tell, Lasine didn't hang out with the other established hunters; he didn't use the blacksmiths' divination services; and he didn't wear talismans or fetishes like the other hunters.

Lasine wasn't magic. He was an athlete.

If you are a good enough athlete, you can run down a warthog. And if your dogs know how to handle an exhausted warthog, you can get a rope around its neck and make it walk back to town. And if you lead it back to town while school is in session, the school director will declare a recess and a big crowd of excited kids will turn your arrival into a parade.

Lasine once got into trouble with the village chief for starting a fire hunt during school hours – one of the hunts pictured below. I'm not sure why the school director didn't get in trouble though. He was the one who declared the impromptu field trip and collected a "meat tax" for the privilege. I, of course, supported the director's decision because it meant that I could get out of class too!

Lasine was constantly on my case for being unable to run like a real man. He was much less successful when he dragged me or my wife and Peace Corps friends along on his hunts, but I/we always got invited back. I like to think I saved a few animals' lives with my ineptness as a magic hunter.

My friend Tom, who is a runner, came to visit. We still failed to chase anything down on the hunt with Tom. But Lasine talked about Tom for months afterwards as if he were the only real American man in existence. Tom was a Peace Corps volunteer in Niger, and his village name was Banya. Lasine's alpha-male dog was coincidentally named Banya too, which really tickled Lasine.

I was very proud of myself once – still am – because I spotted a scorpion climbing up my wall in the candlelight during one of Lasine's evening visits. The scorpion was small, but it was right in front of us. He was incredulous that I had seen it before he did. He basically told me that my "amazing eyesight" made it even sadder that I couldn't run. Works for me...

My entire Peace Corps experience, with all of its ups and downs, would have been worth it if the only good thing that happened was that I got to know Lasine Koné.

***

Here's a boy chasing warthogs past my house. Supposedly warthogs sometimes get mixed in with a herd of cattle and don't realize that they've walked too close to a village. I was in my house with one of my blacksmith friends when we heard commotion outside. My friend saw what was happening and blocked the door "for my protection". All he said was "Dangerous animal!" so I, of course, had to grab my camera and force my way out. I managed to get this picture of a boy giving chase on a warthog and two piglets. The warthogs made it to the scrubby area and escaped.

***

The one boy is helpfully pointing in the direction of the fire started by Lasine Koné. This is the fire hunt that got Lasine in trouble with the village chief, most of these guys are supposed to be in school. I am also supposed to be in school, but the school director really had no choice but to call a field trip. I thought of it as the equivalent of expecting a classroom full of surfers in a California school to sit still for a math lesson while epic surf is happening. The mushroom shaped things are termite mounds (but not the kind that Dluhosh in Used Aliens looks like).

***

The fire approaches and small animals start to emerge. I should point out that people have been burning these grasslands for a thousand years or more. And lightning also starts a lot of fires in the dried grass late in the dry season. So the ecology of this region is adapted to fire, and I suspect that some of the plants are dependent on fire just like some trees in the western U.S. Also, like in the U.S., if fires aren't allowed to burn periodically, the fuels build up and can cause a catastrophic fire. So people burned the grasslands for safety, visibility, and grazing enhancement – as well as for hunting. Our Peace Corps training facility received a visit from a delegation of local chiefs because the property had not been allowed to burn for several years. I think they ended up doing some controlled burns there.

***

At this point, as described in Used Aliens, hares, mongooses, and a small duiker antelope have emerged and most of the boys and their dogs have taken off after them. The duiker fell to a hunter with a gun, but unfortunately I lost the picture I took.

***

This man has some of the optional equipment for those who don't own a gun – a heavy stick for whapping, and a hand-hoe for clubbing. The brightly colored hat could be considered safety gear that might keep him from being shot.

***

The guy in the white shirt has a pair of fishing spears, which are made from a four-foot sharpened length of re-bar attached to wooden handles. It was well over 100F/40C, and the fire wasn't exactly making it cooler. This is HOT work.

***

Rounding up the stragglers… You can see that the guy in gray at center right is dispatching a small rodent. Also notice the snake, which I assume is an African rock python, that they guy at left has tied in a knot. Eating snakes seemed to be controversial, and in Used Aliens the hunters scatter from a large python. I'm not sure if eating snake is some kind of cultural taboo, but I do know that a typical Malian villager is terrified of snakes. They are also afraid of touching frogs because they say a frog might stick permanently to your skin. But I think they have more practical reasons for being afraid of snakes. I also observed fishermen kill large cobras on two occasions, and both times they just tossed the snake into the river. If they wouldn't eat the snake, it seems like they could have at least sold the skin. I was never able to get a good explanation for the rejection of the snakes. Often when I would question things that seemed to have a spiritual element, I would just get "Oh, that's just how it is" as an answer. I think the reason for the non-answers was that knowledge of these things imparts *nyama* (a sort of life force as explained in Used Aliens) that could bring harm to me if my personal *nyama* wasn't adequately prepared – which it obviously wasn't.

***

The school director (left, blue shorts) supervises his students and waits for his consideration.

***

The kid in the yellow shorts seems to be one who thinks that eating snake is a bad idea. An interesting bit of trivia is that the Bambara/Malinké word for "meat" and "mammal" is the same – *sogo*. Snake was not *sogo* in either sense of the word for some folks.

***

Here's my friend "Steve Hansen" with a cane rat, mongoose, and a small rodent of the type that I like to call "snack rats". "Steve" was the acknowledged chief of the village boys. His other nickname was "Dugutigi", which means village chief. His real name is Bougari Traoré. He and his right-hand-man wanted "toubab" names since I had a Malian name (Yacouba Traoré). So I gave him the most toubab-ish name I could think of. I called his right-hand-man Jacko Melendez, just for some diversity.

***

Here you can see that the school director has collected his "commission". The boy on the right has a hare over his shoulder.

***

Snack rat – cook 'em if you got 'em.

***

As described in Used Aliens, the bummed-looking boy is losing his claim on what I think is a mongoose. There were often disputes about whose dog caught the animal first, and in this case, might makes right. The bigger guys are dividing up the meat.

***

This boy has a cane rat – also called a grass cutter or *konyina*. Along with porcupines, they are the best "bush meat" I tasted. Yes, they are a both rodents, but I'm tellin' ya, rodent is good. You can also see a couple of the fishing spears mentioned above.

***

Close-up of a yummy cane rat.

***

As described in Used Aliens (and the excerpt at the end of this book), this is Dantuma Camara. He is a *basitigi*, which essentially means "trouble master", and the elder blacksmith of my village. He is the one who performs divination ceremonies and makes the various potions that contain "life forces" with a specific purpose – such as protection from disease, animal attack, being detected, and avoiding/creating whatever trouble you need. I took this picture on my first day in the village. Dantuma and his family had slaughtered a goat for our welcoming celebration, and he and his *basitigi* apprentice collected the blood to add to various fetish objects. The thing hanging from Dantuma's face is some sort of talisman on a wire that he poked through his cheek. Again, when I asked about it I just got the "that's just how it is" answer. Anyway, this was the point when I realized that my Peace Corps experience was going to be very interesting…

You can see Dantuma practicing sand divination in 2005 in this video on YouTube:

http://www.youtube.com/watch?v=9HGkJSSKmGs

And you can see his younger brother Baba Camara working in their forge here:

http://www.youtube.com/watch?v=lLXLjy8gu0g

***

These guys are the hunters described in Used Aliens. The two guys on the right are full-time hunters (*Donso*), and the rest of them are farmers and cattle herders who also hunt. I was invited when someone came to my house and said that Dantuma had invited me on a hunt and that I should bring any *dolo* that I might have. I had about ¾ of a bottle of rum that I was saving for a special occasion, and this seemed special enough. Not everyone here drank, and I wouldn't say that anyone here is drunk, but a couple of them probably have a nice buzz going – I know I did.

***

Here's a close-up so you can see their jackets. I pixilated their faces because I never got their permission to use their pictures in a project. I suspect that they might be insulted that I did it, but, well, that's just how it is. Plus, since I'm telling you that they are buzzed on rum and honey brew, and the one guy looks like he's about to pull a Dick Cheney on his buddy, I figured I should disguise them. Even though this was 20 years ago...

***

Off to the hunt...

***

This is my friend Braman Camara. He is also a blacksmith, so I think that may be why he is the one lighting the fire. Blacksmiths seem to have all sorts of little ceremonial duties. For this fire I was instructed to go to the back side, which seemed like a pretty good idea with the buzzed gunplay that was planned for the downwind side of the field.

***

Here it goes…

***

Here's the obligatory wall-of-flames close-up picture.

***

Sitting in a tree might have seemed like a good idea, but this guy went home empty handed.

***

What it looks like from the back side.

***

Well, this cane rat is the only thing I saw anyone get in this hunt. And this man had showed up late.

***

Here's the man who was in the tree going home empty handed. I had a feeling that he blamed my presence for his failure, even though he didn't drink any of my rum.

***

This is the same hunter from the fire hunt. He is the only one who we met who had shot a lion. He said he did it in self defense, and that it's not good to kill lions. He may have just been telling us what he thought we wanted to hear, but my blacksmith friends said that this was true. That's the lion skin behind him. We never saw a lion while we were there. My wife took this picture when she was on a health education tour of the villages in our area.

***

Here are a couple of close-ups of one of the locally blacksmith-made guns. I know this gun works because I saw a fisherman shoot an ibis with it from a canoe.

***

This is the "fetish market" in Bamako. This is where you might come with a "prescription" from a *basitigi* to get some ingredients for a fetish – a square inch of lion skin or a smoked monkey hand, for example. The large animal head is a roan antelope as described in Used Aliens (but with its horns on backwards). A close look at the stocks of these vendors made me wonder if there was *anything* that didn't have "magical" powers.

***

This is another vendor in the fetish market area. I had visited these stalls four or five times before I felt comfortable asking to take pictures. I can tell you right now that they DO NOT like having tourists take their pictures without a hefty fee. But after a few non-judgmental visits, the vendors seemed to begin to trust me. And I gave them copies of the pictures, which tourists never do, of course. When I went back in 2005, the fetish market had moved from the corner between the National Assembly and the main Bamako market to a small market a mile up the road. This vendor is looking at my African mammals book and misidentifying a surprisingly high percentage of the animals. I believe that the large skull in front is a hippo.

***

I can't fail to include a hippo picture. Mali means "hippopotamus" in Bambara. This "family" is on a small island in the Niger River near Mopti. Hippos were difficult to spot near my village, but it was common to see their tracks on the river banks. People told me that a famous hunter a hundred years ago had killed almost all the hippos in the region. I always thought of him as Hippo Bill. Jerk. Hippos are supposedly the most

154

dangerous four-legged animal in Africa in terms of numbers of people killed. (The more dangerous animals are the six-legged variety.) So I assume he killed them for this reason.

***

Well, thanks for letting me share these stories and pictures with you! I don't know when or if I'll be going back to Mali again. Peace Corps pulled all of its volunteers out of Mali in 2012 due to the conflicts in the north. I have remained in contact with some of the people in this story through the mail, and as far as I can tell, things there pretty much continue how I remember them.

Recent letters indicate that the country's schools, hospitals, and post offices are functioning. I just hope that the political and military situation stabilizes so that casual visitors like J. Anne and me, and maybe you with your fishing pole, can feel comfortable visiting again. And I'd really like to bring my daughter as proof that my, um, equipment wasn't broken…

***

The author schmoozing the fetish market vendors in Bamako in 1993. Nice pants and fanny pack, dude. (Photo taken by G. L. Doumbia, who also did the artwork for Used Aliens.)

***

Excerpt from the novel Used Aliens

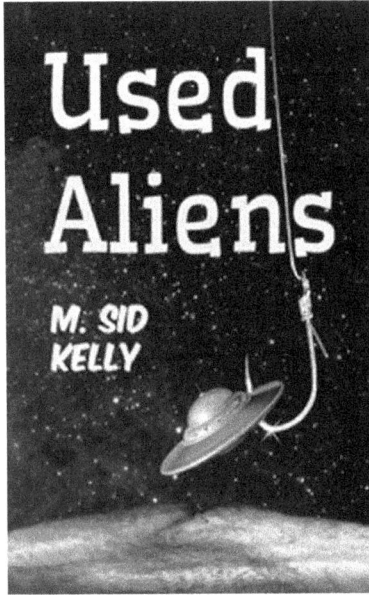

THE FIRE HUNT

Trukk-9 called to Dluhosh. "It looks like stoves are being lit, Dluhosh. Good morning!"

It was before sunrise and the women cooked millet flour porridge as the men were stirring in their beds. Roosters crowed and a donkey brayed.

Fleence said, "Oh, look at that bug!" She had just seen her first butterfly – a big yellow and black swallowtail with blue and red eyespots. She picked out another three or four different species flitting around. "They are everywhere!"

"See? Abundant insectoids can be a beautiful sight," said Buzzy.

Down below, women pulled water from wells to heat for the men. The men did not speak until after bathing. Then everyone wished everyone else a good morning and asked how they'd slept. Young girls with younger girls strapped to their backs pounded corn using wooden mortars and pestles.

"Wow," said Fleence. "That pounding makes it sound like the whole village has a pulse."

Trukk-9 pointed to a family compound at the edge of the village. "That's where the blacksmith family lives. They should be firing up their forge pretty soon. The hunters will stop here before the fire hunt. So we should abduct Numun to have him show us where the boy lives first."

They spotted Numun walking with an apprentice boy toward the forge.

"I can probably grab them both – might as well. Is anyone looking?" asked Dluhosh.

Stick.E said, "I'm pretty sure it's all clear."

Dluhosh piloted his ship over Numun and his apprentice, opened the hatch, and grabbed them with the grabber beam. And Numun and his nephew became the first Dirtlings ever legally abducted onto an alien ship.

Numun and the apprentice sat on the abductee platform with the containment dome around them. They were then exposed to the calming agent. Numun was immobilized as the probaluation apparatus rose from the floor behind him. The ship's computer uploaded a wealth of data about Numun, including a complete sequencing of his DNA. The probaluation had given him a thorough physical exam and cured him of various minor diseases and injuries, including the chronic pain in his shoulder. And during his probaluation, many dead parasitic worms passed from the boy. Dluhosh cleaned up the worms and added them to the duplicator matter conversion supply.

Fleence reached for her egocite and readied it for her first psychological test. She placed the small metallic ball on the platform next to the handsome man, and then Dluhosh lifted the containment field.

The egocite ingot did not change.

Dluhosh said, "Hello, my name is Dluhosh-10 and this is my partner, Fleence-18. We have come from elsewhere in the galaxy as part of a team that is evaluating Dirt for possible inclusion in our Galactic Pool. We apologize for our rudeness in snatching you up like this, and we especially apologize for probaluating you like that. However, the probaluation has provided us with invaluable data, has cured you of several existing medical problems, and has vaccinated you against several others."

Numun said, "Right on!"

Then Trukk-9's voice and image came over the video display. "Hello Numun! How are you? How are your children? How did you sleep? How is your wife? I hope your health is good! You and your work! You and the hammering of hot iron! You are Numun!"

"Right on!" Numun was otherwise lost for words.

Trukk-9 continued. "Numun, I apologize for my colleagues and their abrupt introductions. I would go around and introduce everyone, but we don't have the time. And besides, we are going to wipe your memory of this. You will get to keep your new health though."

"You and your work!" said Numun.

"Um... Right on!" said Trukk-9. "So Numun, we've been following you and your family for a few months now. You have become an example of a typical Dirt family for the

159

education of the people of our galactic family. I personally hope that I get to meet you again someday. Anyway, a few weeks ago you counseled a woman who has a son that was to be hired out to the woman's brother-in-law. We would like to meet this boy."

"Do you mean the tall boy?" asked Numun.

"We don't know. We have only seen his mother."

"It is probably Yacouba that you seek. I can show you where he is."

"Were you able to help the woman keep the boy?" asked Trukk-9.

"Well, my brother performed some sacrifices with a chicken and kola nuts, and he said words. I am not allowed to witness his work, but my brother is very powerful. Now that you have arrived I think that he has been successful."

"Of course. I like your brother very much," replied Trukk-9

Numun pointed the way to the clay quarry where Yacouba worked before school making bricks for repairs to his family's granary.

Numun said, "That is the boy. He is a very bright and respectful boy, but he is also very strong. His family is in debt, and they can hire him out to work in the gold mines for enough to pay off the creditors."

"Can I ask a question?" said Fleence. "Like this boy – are people forced to work off the debts of other people? Are people made to serve others without a choice?"

"Oh yes, that sort of thing happens," replied Numun.

"Thank you."

Trukk-9 continued. "Will Yacouba be at the fire hunt today? And do you think that if he became a very successful hunter that his uncle might not send him away?"

Numun said, "Yes. Especially if he could get enough

meat to pay off the debt..."

Stick.E said, "There are some people coming."

"Okay, Numun," said Trukk-9, "we are going to place you back where we found you. You will go unconscious for a second as we erase your memory of this encounter. You will probably be a little disoriented and wonder how you came to be sitting down. I apologize for that. Greet the people!"

"Right on! They will hear it! But wait, can I get you to do your disease cure on my children, and my friend's children?"

"No. I'm sorry, but the rules do not allow gratuitous disease curing," said Dluhosh.

Numun and his apprentice found themselves sitting face to face on the ground next to the forge. Numun yelled something and shook his finger at the boy. The boy ran into the forge shed.

"Well, what do you think? Can we intervene on behalf of the boy?" asked Trukk-9 of Dluhosh.

Buzzy replied, "Slavery is a Level-1 checklist item…"

"Well, that's a valid point. And you've already uncovered several other checklist items here. There's still much we can learn from this place…" replied Dluhosh. "Why – what do you have in mind?"

"I think we should get a bunch of animals for Yacouba. Stick here can easily grab up whatever we can find before the hunt. Then he can make the animals run out of the grass right to Yacouba's feet, and we can even help kill the animals for him. We can load him up with meat."

"Alright, I think intervention in this case is legitimate," said Dluhosh.

***

As they flew over the river Dee yelled, "Flippo! I see a flippo!"

Buzzy said, "Yes, that does appear to be a hippopotamus. But I do not know whether the people eat them."

"Well, that's a heck of a lot of meat, Cousin. I think we should try."

"Yes, we should," said Trukk-9. "Can you manage that thing, Stick?"

Stick maxed out all of his grabber beams while pulling the hippo up through the cargo hold hatch. Dee hit it with a mega-dose of calming agent.

"Man, I think this sucker is immune to calming agent! He's really tearing things up in there. Wow! Look at those teeth! I don't think we can keep him Skip."

So Stick returned the hippo to the river.

"HAAAHAAA! That was awesome Stick, but I don't think you needed to flip him. Dang, that is one pissed off flippopotamus!"

The ships continued to the other side of the river. They found a troop of baboons on a small hill, and grabbed a half dozen. Then they spotted a small duiker antelope and grabbed it. They found a mother warthog digging up roots with two piglets, and grabbed the three of them. Down in a dry gulch they grabbed an entire flock of wild Guinea fowl, and also a large rock python and Nile monitor lizard that had been attracted by the birds.

And then they spotted a big prize. It was a bull roan antelope with a harem of females with calves.

"Stick, can you grab a herd of beasts that big?" asked Trukk-9.

"If you have room for them…"

"Dee, how's the cargo hold looking?"

"Well Skip, it's pretty crazy in there. But if I give them

enough calming agent there should be room to squeeze 'em in! They'll have to cuddle up, but I think it will do them some good. I might have to go in and join them."

"Make it be. Snag them and let's get back to the village."

***

The ships arrived back at the village as a group of hunters entered the blacksmith compound. The hunters greeted Numun's brother, and he replied with 'Right on!' many times.

One of the hunters – the one with the most shotgun shells, fetish pouches, mirrors, and animal parts hanging from his clothes – carried a ten-liter yellow plastic jug of a honey brew that he had already been sampling. He passed it around to the other hunters finally.

Fleence was distracted by the hunters. They were calm and majestic and seemed to own their space, yet none of them seemed to be posturing. Dluhosh noticed a flicker of unusual life sign readings from Fleence on his monitor. Her heart rate and skin temperature were both elevated. He looked at her and she appeared flushed, but otherwise healthy and alert.

The elder blacksmith smoothed out a patch of sand and drew small clusters of short parallel lines in it. Then he bit off a piece of kola nut and tossed the remaining piece of nut onto the patterned sand. Then he spit some of the chewed kola nut onto the pattern. He consulted a notebook with similar patterns drawn in it. He then drew some lines on a small copper plate with a piece of charcoal. He looked up at the eager hunters.

"I can't tell," he said. "It's neutral. The hunt could go either way."

The hunters seemed satisfied with that prophecy, and they all took another swig of the brew.

***

People gathered on the river floodplain where the

hunters were going to light the grass fire. The boys and young men arrived with their dogs, machetes, clubs, slingshots, knives, rope, and sacks. Most of the adult hunters carried shotguns of varying quality – the finest being made by famous local blacksmiths. A couple of the hunters had locally-made muzzle-loaders as well.

Three of the lower-ranking hunters walked to the upwind side of the tall grass field and lit a small fire. They took bundles of flaming grass and jogged along the windward edge of the field, lighting new grass as they went. The wind whipped the flames into a fast-moving wall. The remaining hunters, every boy and his dog in the village, and the two village school teachers, waited in a clearing about a kilometer downwind.

The first creatures to emerge from the grass were hares. Most of the dogs and small boys ran off after these. The hares fought the dogs for their lives, the dogs fought each other for the hares, then the boys fought the dogs for the hares, and then boys fought each other for the hares and portions thereof. Then the school teachers, who had let the boys out of class, took what they wanted.

Small rodents scampered out all along the edge of the grass. Older boys killed these with sticks and collected them in their sacks as they waited for larger animals to emerge.

Trukk-9 located the boy. Then he instructed Dee to lower their cloaked ship into the grass ahead of the fire. "Okay, Stick, start sending the animals out through the grass to the boy. Try to get them to emerge from the grass and die at his feet, but make it look like the boy is killing them! Fire at will!"

Stick.E started with the Guinea fowl to warm the boy up. He squeezed each one to death as he shoved them through the grass. Yacouba appeared to swat expertly with his cane as the birds piled up.

164

Then Stick.E sent the warthogs in, strangling the mother as he shoved her out of the grass. Yacouba took a wild swing with his hand-hoe club, but seemed to deliver a perfect blow.

As soon as the other boys had caught the piglets, Stick.E shoved the rock python out. Everyone scattered, but the snake lay dead where Yacouba had been.

Based on this feedback, Stick.E decided against using the big lizard. So he sent the small duiker antelope out next. A hunter took a shot at the duiker and instead shot the pinky and ring finger from Yacouba's left hand.

Then Stick.E shoved out the entire family of roan antelopes with the baboons clinging to their backs. The antelope heard 'gave itself' to Yacouba where he lay on the ground being tended to by the teachers and the other boys. The baboons managed to get the hell out of there.

Dee piloted the ship up and over the grass to get a better look at the result. They saw the injured boy.

"Oh no! Now what do we do, Dluhosh?" asked a panicked Trukk-9.

"Well, we don't have enough space on my platform to abduct everybody at once. I can probably take five. How many can you take over there, Trukk-9?" asked Dluhosh.

"We can probably take twenty if we get rid of the big lizard in the cargo hold, but my ship isn't equipped to probaluate them or erase their memories. Oh, what have I done?" cried Trukk-9.

"I'd say you just shot that boy out of slavery for good, Skip! He can't work in a goldmine now."

"That's a good point. It is very very mysterious how these things work out," said Trukk-9. He felt better already.

***

A crowd gathered at the chief's compound to hear the

story and witness the arrival of the meat. Volunteers butchered the beasts and carried the pieces to the village by bike and by back.

The careless hunter explained that the duiker had redirected the shot away from itself. "They have the most powerful life force in the bush – everyone knows that. How else could such a defenseless animal survive amongst lions and hyenas?" he pleaded.

A few of the chief's councilors were of the opinion that the hunter hadn't taken care to prepare his own life force – otherwise he might have missed the duiker but not hit Yacouba. The chief decided that the guilty hunter should pay Yacouba's medical bills and buy his family one-hundred kilos of rice and condiments for the meat.

The chief's intermediary announced the verdict. Everyone agreed that this was adequate, and the matter was settled.

Buzzy said, "We got several items on that: a legal proceeding with a verdict; application of first aid using traditional medicine; food gathering techniques; animistic beliefs with application of magic and divination; and – depending on which checklist you use – we got slavery and drunken use of weaponry."

"Well, that was a good haul, I'd say," said Trukk-9.

Dluhosh said, "My priority is still to focus on the bad stuff, but I agree that we've done well so far."

"Thanks, Dluhosh," said Trukk-9, "I'm feeling better about being able to work with you to our mutual benefit. Anyway, I really want to do some of the wildest sort of stuff that Stick and his grabber beams can do with our favorite guy. It's Friday, so chances are he'll be fishing tomorrow."

***

APPENDICES

Other books by the author:

Used Aliens (A satirical comedy about a botched alien invasion of Earth and the inept galactic politicians who plotted it. Contains more bass fishing and visits to Mali than most sci-fi stories…)

Available at: http://www.amazon.com/dp/B00BJ602QQ

Video clips from 2005:

The "elephant-killing" cichlid: http://youtu.be/fz-dP8QqPAs

A community fishing event: http://youtu.be/sQ90JZTI6zQ

Women fishing and large fruit bats:
http://youtu.be/vDUZwQ1Txxg

Artisanal gold mining on Niger River:
http://youtu.be/eEYDNW_upN8

Cast netting from canoe: http://youtu.be/Xkkx8zGWZNM

Exploring Le Fié River: http://youtu.be/rj_l0PnkG_c

Blacksmiths working in forge: http://youtu.be/lLXLjy8gu0g

-My YouTube channel also contains several other videos from Mali that aren't as closely related to this topic, as well as a couple hundred various short nature videos (with no advertising). http://youtube.com/user/HumboldtMike

TIGERFISH!

Useful references:

West African Freshwater Fish by Holden and Reed. Published by Longman Group 1972

Biodiversity Dynamics and Conservation – The Freshwater Fish of Tropical Arica by Christian Léveque. Published by Cambridge University Press, 1997

The Niger River Basin – A vision for Sustainable Management. Published by The World Bank

Somono Bala of the Upper Niger by David Conrad. Published by Brill, 2002

The Mandé Blacksmiths: Knowledge, Power, and Art in West Africa by Patrick McNaughton. Published by Indiana University Press, 1993

The Collins Field Guide to the Birds of West Africa. Published by The Stephen Greene Press, 1977

Review of the Present State of Knowledge of Environment, Fish Stocks, and Fisheries of the Niger River by Raymond Lae, et al.

Petit Dictionaire Bambara-Francais Francais-Bambara by Pere Charles Bailleul. Published by Avebury Publishing, 1981

Ichtyologie et Peche by Dr. F. D. Dansoko. Published by the *Ministere de l'Environment et de l'Elevage*, Republic of Mali, 1990

www.ingramcontent.com/pod-product-compliance
Lightning Source LLC
Chambersburg PA
CBHW061145040426
42445CB00013B/1555